DOE/EA-1745

I0468861

FINAL ENVIRONMENTAL ASSESSMENT

FOR THE

BLAST FURNACE GAS FLARE CAPTURE PROJECT AT THE ARCELORMITTAL USA, INC. INDIANA HARBOR STEEL MILL, EAST CHICAGO, INDIANA

U.S. Department of Energy
National Energy Technology Laboratory

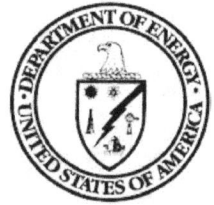 

August 2010

COVER SHEET

Responsible Agency: U.S. Department of Energy (DOE)

Title: *Final Environmental Assessment for the Blast Furnace Gas Flare Capture Project at the ArcelorMittal USA, Inc. Indiana Harbor Steel Mill, East Chicago, Indiana* (DOE/EA-1745)

Contact: For additional copies or more information about this environmental assessment (EA), please contact:

> Mr. Mark W. Lusk
> U.S. Department of Energy
> National Energy Technology Laboratory
> P.O. Box 880, MS B07
> 3610 Collins Ferry Road
> Morgantown, West Virginia 26507-0880
> Facsimile: (304) 285-4403
> E-mail: mark.lusk@netl.doe.gov

Abstract: DOE prepared this EA to evaluate the potential environmental consequences of providing a financial assistance grant under the American Recovery and Reinvestment Act of 2009 to ArcelorMittal USA, Inc. (ArcelorMittal) to construct and operate a boiler to capture blast furnace waste gas and convert it into electricity.

DOE's Proposed Action is to provide $31.5 million in financial assistance in a cost-sharing arrangement with the project proponent, ArcelorMittal. The total cost of the proposed project would be about $63.2 million. ArcelorMittal's project involves construction and operation of a blast furnace gas recovery boiler to capture and use 46 billion cubic feet of blast furnace gas per year. ArcelorMittal would use the gas, which it currently burns and releases to the atmosphere, to generate electricity for use at the plant.

This EA evaluates 14 resource areas and identifies no significant adverse environmental impacts for the proposed project. The project could result in beneficial impacts to the nation's energy efficiency and the local economy. In addition to adding and retaining jobs in the East Chicago area, the project would use waste energy in blast furnace gas to generate electricity. The electricity would replace the same amount of electricity ArcelorMittal purchases from utilities that use conventional power-generating sources such as coal-fired power plants.

Availability: The EA is available on DOE's National Energy Technology Laboratory (NETL) website at http://www.netl.doe.gov/publications/others/nepa/ea.html.

ACRONYMS AND ABBREVIATIONS

CFR   *Code of Federal Regulations*

DOE   U.S. Department of Energy

EA   environmental assessment

EPA   U.S. Environmental Protection Agency

FWS   U.S. Fish and Wildlife Service

FR   *Federal Register*

NEPA   National Environmental Policy Act of 1969, as amended

NETL   National Energy Technology Laboratory

PM_{10} particulate matter with median aerodynamic diameter of 10 micrometers or less

$PM_{2.5}$ particulate matter with median aerodynamic diameter of 2.5 micrometers or less

Stat.   *United States Statutes at Large*

U.S.C.   *United States Code*

Note: Numbers in this EA generally have been rounded to two or three significant figures. Therefore, some total values might not equal the actual sums of the values.

CONTENTS

LIST OF TABLES

LIST OF FIGURES

APPENDIXES

SUMMARY

The U.S. Department of Energy (DOE or the Department) proposes to award a financial assistance grant under the American Recovery and Reinvestment Act of 2009 (Recovery Act) to ArcelorMittal USA, Inc. (ArcelorMittal) for its proposed project. The proposed project would construct and operate a blast furnace gas recovery boiler and supporting infrastructure at ArcelorMittal's Indiana Harbor Steel Mill in East Chicago, Indiana. The mill occupies about 3,400 acres. DOE's Proposed Action is to provide ArcelorMittal with a $31.5 million grant in a cost-sharing arrangement. The total cost of site preparation, equipment installation, and start-up of the proposed project would be about $63.2 million.

At present, ArcelorMittal burns about 22 percent of the blast furnace gas from Indiana Harbor operations before releasing it to the atmosphere through an exhaust stack, a process called *flaring*. The company uses the remaining 78 percent of the gas to power boilers. The proposed project would result in a reduction of the amount of waste gas that is flared. The proposed project would use the waste gas to power a new 80-percent efficient boiler to produce 350,000 pounds of steam per hour, and then use the steam to drive existing turbines to generate electricity. The boiler would generate about 38 megawatts of electricity (333,000 megawatt-hours per year), enough to power 30,000 homes.

DOE evaluated 14 environmental resource categories and identified no significant adverse impacts from the proposed project. For nine of the resource categories DOE determined there would be no impacts or the potential impacts would be small, temporary, or both and therefore did not carry those forward for additional analysis. DOE focused its analyses on those resources that could require new or amended permits, have the potential for significant impacts or controversy, or typically interest the public, such as socioeconomics and occupational health and safety. DOE performed more detailed analyses of potential impacts on air quality, water resources, waste, socioeconomics, and occupational health and safety. The following paragraphs summarize the analyses.

Air Quality. The proposed project would have the beneficial impact of recovering waste energy and converting it into electricity for use at the steel mill. This would allow ArcelorMittal to purchase less electricity from regional power plants, which could reduce pollutant emissions from conventional power-generating sources that use fossil fuels.

Air emissions during construction for the proposed project would include combustion emissions from vehicles and heavy-duty equipment and fugitive dust from site preparation activities. These emissions would have short-term adverse impacts that ArcelorMittal could mitigate through best management practices such as soil stabilization and watering of exposed soils. Fugitive dust emissions would cease on completion of construction, so long-term impacts would be negligible.

Air emissions during operations would be about the same as current emissions, with the exception of minimal increases in nitrogen oxides and carbon monoxide. The proposed project would generate about 330,000 megawatt-hours per year of electricity (enough to serve about 30,000 households), and there would be a slight increase of greenhouse gas emissions on the site.

Water Resources. The Indiana Harbor Steel Mill is located within the Grand Calumet River watershed. The proposed project would neither contribute to the existing contamination nor impede cleanup activities.

The proposed project would use water from Indiana Harbor Steel Mill's existing intakes in Lake Michigan. ArcelorMittal would treat wastewater in the existing onsite secondary treatment plant as appropriate. The main source of wastewater would be from boiler blowdown, which contains carbonites and scaling materials. The proposed project would have a small impact on the quantity of wastewater the steel mill discharges into the Grand Calumet River, and there would be no change in the quality of that wastewater. The current ArcelorMittal National Pollutant Discharge Elimination System permit would not require modification.

Waste. Construction for the proposed project would generate construction-related debris such as wood, metal, and concrete. ArcelorMittal would recycle some of this waste and ship the remainder to a permitted commercial landfill in Newton County, Indiana. During normal operations, ArcelorMittal would generate miscellaneous municipal wastes (for example, wood, paper, garbage, and absorbents) and a minor amount of hazardous waste (caustic and toxic chemicals from water testing) from the laboratory at the facility that would not affect regional landfills or treatment plants.

Socioeconomics. The proposed project would have the beneficial impact of creating new direct and indirect jobs during construction, aiding in the retention of jobs in a critical manufacturing process, and stimulating the economic base of the community. DOE expects that members of the community's existing labor force would fill the new jobs, so there would be no adverse impacts to existing infrastructure or social services.

1. INTRODUCTION

As part of the American Recovery and Reinvestment Act of 2009 (the Recovery Act; Public Law 111-5, 123 Stat. 115), the National Energy Technology Laboratory (NETL), on behalf of the Office of Energy Efficiency and Renewable Energy's Industrial Technologies Program, is providing up to $156 million in federal funding for competitively awarded grants for the deployment of projects for district energy systems, combined heat and power systems, waste energy recovery systems, and energy-efficient industrial equipment and processes at single or multiple installations and sites. The funding of the selected projects requires compliance with the National Environmental Policy Act of 1969 (NEPA; 42 U.S.C. 4321 et seq.), Council on Environmental Quality regulations (40 CFR Parts 1500 to 1508), and the NEPA implementing procedures of the U.S. Department of Energy (DOE or the Department) (10 CFR Part 1021).

To comply with NEPA, DOE prepared this *Final Environmental Assessment for the Blast Furnace Gas Flare Capture Project at the ArcelorMittal USA, Inc. Indiana Harbor Steel Mill, East Chicago, Indiana* (EA). This EA examines the potential environmental impacts of DOE's Proposed Action, providing financial assistance, and the ArcelorMittal USA, Inc. (ArcelorMittal) proposed project, construction and operation of a waste energy recovery facility at its Indiana Harbor Steel Mill (Indiana Harbor) in East Chicago, Lake County, Indiana. The proposed facility would capture and process 22 percent of the waste blast furnace gas ArcelorMittal currently burns and releases to the atmosphere. ArcelorMittal would use the waste gas to produce electricity for use in its Indiana Harbor Steel Mill operations. The EA also examines the No-Action Alternative, under which DOE assumes that, because of its denial of financial assistance, ArcelorMittal would not proceed with the project.

This chapter explains NEPA and related regulations (Section 1.1), the background of the Industrial Technologies Program (Section 1.2), the Department's purpose and need for action (Section 1.3), and the environmental resources DOE did not carry forward to detailed analysis (Section 1.4). Chapter 2 discusses DOE's Proposed Action, ArcelorMittal's proposed project, the No-Action Alternative, and DOE's Alternative Actions. Chapter 3 details the affected environment and the potential environmental consequences of the proposed project and of the No-Action Alternative and considers resource commitments. Chapter 4 addresses cumulative impacts, and Chapter 5 provides DOE's conclusions from the analyses. Chapter 6 lists the references for this document. Appendix A contains the distribution list, and Appendix B contains correspondence between DOE and the Indiana Division of Historic Preservation and Archaeology.

1.1 National Environmental Policy Act and Related Regulations

In accordance with its NEPA implementing procedures, DOE must evaluate the potential environmental impacts of funding decisions. Therefore, this EA examines the potential direct, indirect, and cumulative environmental impacts of the proposed project and of the No-Action Alternative. The No-Action Alternative provides a basis of comparison between the proposed project's impacts and those that would occur if DOE did not provide funding to support the construction and operation of a blast furnace gas waste energy recovery boiler at the Indiana Harbor Steel Mill.

DOE must comply with the requirements of NEPA before it can make a final decision to proceed with a proposed federal action that could cause adverse impacts to human health or the environment. This EA fulfills DOE's obligations under NEPA and provides DOE with the information necessary to make an informed decision about the construction and operation of an efficient boiler that would produce electricity through the recovery of the waste energy in blast furnace gas.

1.2 Background of the Industrial Technologies Program

DOE's National Energy Technology Laboratory manages the research and development portfolio of the Industrial Technologies Program for the Office of Energy Efficiency and Renewable Energy. The mission of the Industrial Technologies Program is to establish U.S. industry as a world leader in energy efficiency and productivity. The program leads the national effort to reduce industrial energy intensity and carbon emissions, and strives to transform the way U.S. industry uses energy by supporting cost-shared research and development that addresses the top energy challenges facing industry. In addition, the Industrial Technologies Program fosters the adoption of advanced technologies and energy management best practices to produce meaningful progress in reducing industrial energy intensity.

Congress appropriated significant funding for the Industrial Technologies Program in the Recovery Act to stimulate the economy and reduce unemployment in addition to furthering the objectives of the existing program. DOE solicited applications for this funding by issuing a competitive Funding Opportunity Announcement (DE-FOA-0000044), *Recovery Act: Deployment of Combined Heat and Power (CHP) Systems, District Energy Systems, Waste Energy Recovery Systems, and Efficient Industrial Equipment,* in June 2009. The announcement invited applications in four areas of interest:

- Area of Interest 1 – Combined Heat and Power; the generation of electric energy and heat in a single, integrated system, with an overall thermal efficiency of 60 percent or greater on a higher-heating-value basis.

- Area of Interest 2 – District Energy Systems; systems providing thermal energy from a renewable energy source, thermal energy source, or highly efficient technology to more than one building or fixed energy-consuming use from one or more thermal energy production facilities through pipes or other means to provide space heating, space conditioning, hot water, steam, compression, process energy, or other end uses.

- Area of Interest 3 – Industrial Waste Energy Recovery; the collection and reuse of energy from sources such as exhaust heat or flared gas from any industrial process; waste gas or industrial tail gas that would otherwise be flared, incinerated, or vented; or a pressure drop in any gas, excluding any pressure drop to a condenser that subsequently vents the resulting heat.

- Area of Interest 4 – Efficient Industrial Equipment; any proven commercially available technology that can provide a minimum 25-percent efficiency improvement to the industrial sector.

DOE announced its selections on November 3, 2009, with multiple awards in three of the four areas of interest. DOE selected nine projects based on the evaluation criteria in the funding opportunity announcement and gave special consideration to projects that promoted the objectives of the Recovery Act, specifically job preservation or creation and economic recovery in an expeditious manner.

The proposed project covered in this EA, to construct and operate a blast furnace gas recovery boiler at the Indiana Harbor Steel Mill, East Chicago, Indiana, was one of the nine projects DOE selected for funding. DOE's Proposed Action would provide $31.5 million in financial assistance under a cost-sharing arrangement with ArcelorMittal. The total cost of the proposed project would be about $63.2 million (ArcelorMittal undated).

1.3 Purpose and Need for DOE Action

The purpose of the Proposed Action is to support the mission of DOE's Industrial Technologies Program and the goals of the Recovery Act. The mission of the Industrial Technologies Program is to have U.S. industry lead the world in energy efficiency and productivity. The Program leads the national effort to reduce industrial energy intensity and carbon emissions, and strives to transform the way U.S. industry uses energy by supporting cost-shared research and development that addresses the top energy challenges facing industry. Additionally, the Program fosters the adoption of today's advanced technologies and energy management best practices to produce meaningful progress in reducing industrial energy intensity.

The Industrial Technologies Program's three-part strategy pursues this mission by:

- Sponsoring research, development, and demonstration of industry-specific and crosscutting technologies to reduce energy and carbon intensity;

- Conducting technology delivery activities to help plants access today's technology and management practices; and

- Promoting a corporate culture of energy efficiency and carbon management within industry.

To align with its mission, the program has established a goal of achieving a 25-percent reduction in industrial energy intensity by 2017, guided by the *Energy Policy Act of 2005*. The strategy also calls for an 18-percent reduction in U.S. carbon intensity by 2012. The Department seeks to identify projects and technologies that it can fund to meet this goal.

In June 2009, DOE initiated a process to identify suitable projects by issuing Funding Opportunity Announcement DE-FOA-00000044, *Recovery Act: Deployment of Combined Heat and Power (CHP) Systems, District Energy Systems, Waste Energy Recovery Systems, and Efficient Industrial Equipment.* The Recovery Act funds this Funding Opportunity Announcement.

The Recovery Act seeks to create jobs, restore economic growth, and strengthen America's middle class through measures that modernize the nation's infrastructure, enhance America's energy independence, expand educational opportunities, preserve and improve affordable health care, provide tax relief, and protect those in greatest need. Provision of funds under this Funding Opportunity Announcement would achieve these objectives.

The capital cost of new equipment is often a roadblock for use of more efficient equipment and processes. Although the newer technologies would provide lower energy requirements and operating costs, the payback period for some technologies does not meet internal business goals. DOE's provision of financial assistance allows companies to reduce the payback period, making these new technologies an acceptable option for them.

1.4 Environmental Resources Not Carried Forward

Chapter 3 of this EA describes the affected environment and examines the potential environmental impacts of the proposed project and the No-Action Alternative for the following resource areas:

- Air quality,
- Water resources,
- Waste,
- Socioeconomics, and
- Occupational health and safety.

The focus of the more detailed analyses in Chapter 3 is on those resources that could require new or amended permits, have the potential for significant impacts or controversy, or typically interest the public, such as socioeconomics and occupational health and safety.

DOE EAs also commonly address the environmental resource areas listed in Table 1-1. However, in an effort to streamline the NEPA process and enable a timely award to the selected project, DOE did not examine the resource areas in the table at the same level of detail as the above-mentioned five areas. Table 1-1 describes the Department's evaluation of these resource areas. In each case, there would be no impacts or the potential impacts would be small or temporary in nature, or both. Therefore, DOE determined that further analysis is unnecessary.

In terms of the No-Action Alternative, the impacts Table 1-1 lists would not occur because DOE assumes the proposed project would not proceed.

Table 1-1. Environmental resource areas with no, small, or temporary impacts.

Environmental resource area	Impact consideration and conclusions
Geology and soils	The Indiana Harbor site has served as a heavy industrial facility for more than 100 years. There has been no record of geologic events or site stability issues. ArcelorMittal would construct the proposed boiler on 0.4 acre of previously disturbed land near an existing boilerhouse. The project would require minimal site preparation. The proposed construction site is flat, so potential runoff and sedimentation considerations would be minimal (Whalen 2009).
Land use	Construction and operation of the proposed project would occur within Indiana Harbor Steel Mill's existing site boundary. The site occupies about 3,400 acres in total. There would be no changes to adjacent land uses and the onsite land use related to the proposed project would be consistent with ongoing operations. The proposed project would involve approximately 0.4 acre of previously disturbed land (Whalen 2009).
Aesthetics and visual resources	The proposed project would be similar in appearance to existing Indiana Harbor structures and would not alter or result in major changes or variations to the types of views seen from within the site or at locations adjacent to the site (Whalen 2009).
Noise	The proposed project is not close to the site boundary, so DOE does not expect noise levels from construction and operation to exceed the noise levels of current Indiana Harbor operations. The primary sources of noise would be large steam vents and the fan housing and drive. The safety valves would have large silencers on them, and the fan and drives would have noise insulation. The estimated noise level of the proposed boiler would be 85 A-weighted decibels at about 5 feet. The nearest nonindustrial receptors would be at a marina, boat casino, and hotel complex about 2 miles from the boiler site (Seaman 2010a).
Biological resources	There would be small but temporary impacts to wildlife on or near the proposed project site during the construction phase. Wildlife could be displaced from the area due to the presence of people, vehicles, and operating equipment, and in some circumstances could be killed by cars and construction equipment. Similar impacts could also occur during the operations phase. DOE reviewed the list of federally threatened and endangered species on the U.S. Fish and Wildlife Service (FWS) website (FWS 2010). The endangered Indiana bat (*Myotis sodalis*) and Karner blue butterfly (*Lycaeides melissa samuelis*) occur in Lake County as well as the threatened Pitcher's thistle (*Cirsium pitcheri*) and Mead's milkweed (*Asclepias meadii*). DOE compared the habitat requirements for the listed species with the habitat available within the proposed project site and concluded that no suitable habitat exists to support any of the listed species. DOE determined that there would be no effect on federally threatened or endangered species. DOE received telephone concurrence from the Midwest Region FWS office (Craig 2010) about the species list and concurrence with DOE's determination of no effect.

Table 1-1. Environmental resource areas with no, small, or temporary impacts (continued).

Environmental resource area	Impact consideration and conclusions
Historic and cultural resources	DOE identified properties listed on the *National Register of Historic Places* in East Chicago, Lake County, Indiana. DOE determined that there would be no effects on historic properties because construction would occur more than 2 miles from any listed property on previously disturbed land within the 3,400 acres of the Indiana Harbor site. The Indiana Deputy State Historic Preservation Officer agreed with DOE's determination. Appendix B contains copies of applicable correspondence.
Environmental justice	Executive Order 12898, "Federal Actions to Address Environmental Justice in Minority Populations and Low-Income Populations," directs federal agencies to address environmental and human health considerations in minority and low-income communities. The evaluation of impacts to environmental justice is dependent on determining if high and adverse impacts from the proposed project would disproportionally affect any low-income or minority group in the affected community. DOE determined that no high and adverse impacts would occur to any member of the community. Therefore, DOE also determined there would be no adverse and disproportionate impacts to minority or low-income populations. Section 3.4.1 discusses demographic information for the East Chicago area.
Transportation	Small temporary increases in daily traffic to and from the Indiana Harbor Steel Mill could occur during construction for the proposed project. There would not be a long-term permanent increase in daily traffic from the operation of the proposed plant. Existing public roads are sufficient for accessing the Indiana Harbor site; existing onsite roads are sufficient for accessing the proposed project site (Whalen 2009).
Utilities, energy, and materials	Production of 38 megawatts of electricity would result in small reductions in the use of electricity by the steel mill in comparison with current use. DOE reviewed the local capacities for water, sewer, electricity, and natural gas and found them to be sufficient to support the needs for construction and operation of the proposed boiler. There are no unique materials necessary to manufacture, install, or operate the proposed project.

1.5 Consultations and Public Comment Response Process

DOE issued the Draft EA for comment on June 21, 2010, and advertised its release in the *Northwest Indiana Times* on June 21, 22, and 23. In addition, the Department sent a copy for public review to the East Chicago and Lake County public libraries. The Department established a 15-day public comment period that began June 21, 2010, and ended July 5, 2010, and announced it would accept comments by mail, email, or facsimile. Before the release of the EA for public comment, DOE sent project information to the Indiana Division of Historic Preservation and Archaeology for their consideration, as discussed below. Further, DOE consulted with the FWS.

1.5.1 CONSULTATIONS

Indiana Division of Historic Preservation and Archaeology

On March 17, 2010, DOE sent a formal consultation letter to the Indiana Division of Historic Preservation and Archaeology in accordance with the review requirements of Section 106 of the National Historic Preservation Act, as amended (16 U.S.C. 470 et seq.), and implementing regulations at 36 CFR Part 800. The letter detailed DOE's investigation of nearby historic properties and concluded that no historic properties would be affected by the proposed project.

The Division of Historic Preservation and Archaeology responded on April 19, 2010, and concurred with DOE's finding. Appendix B contains copies of both letters.

U.S. Fish and Wildlife Service, Midwest Region

As Table 1-1 details, DOE examined the FWS list of federally threatened and endangered species and concluded the proposed project would have no effect on listed species. The Department received telephone concurrence from the Midwest Region FWS office (Craig 2010) about the species list and DOE's determination of no effect.

1.5.2 COMMENT-RESPONSE PROCESS

DOE received no comments on the Draft EA.

2. DOE PROPOSED ACTION AND ALTERNATIVES

This chapter describes DOE's Proposed Action (Section 2.1), ArcelorMittal's proposed project (Section 2.2), the No-Action Alternative (Section 2.3), and DOE Alternative Actions (Section 2.4).

2.1 DOE's Proposed Action

DOE's Proposed Action would provide a financial assistance grant to facilitate the construction and operation of a waste energy recovery boiler and related infrastructure that would capture waste blast furnace gas to generate electricity. DOE would award a Recovery Act grant of $31.5 million in a cost-sharing arrangement with ArcelorMittal, which estimates the total cost of its project to be about $63.2 million (ArcelorMittal undated).

2.2 ArcelorMittal's Proposed Project

ArcelorMittal's proposed project would install and operate a waste energy recovery facility that would capture and use 46 billion cubic feet per year of blast furnace gas to generate electricity at its Indiana Harbor Steel Mill. The energy content of the blast furnace gas is currently wasted when it is burned and released to the atmosphere. ArcelorMittal would build the facility at its Mill located on Lake Michigan in East Chicago, Indiana, about 20 miles southeast of Chicago. Figure 2-1 provides a regional map showing the approximate location of East Chicago.

The Indiana Harbor Steel Mill is the largest steel mill in North America and has the largest blast furnace. Indiana Harbor was the location of the Inland Steel Company from 1906 until it was sold in 1998 to Ispat International, which later became Mittal Steel, now ArcelorMittal. The 3,400-acre Indiana Harbor site is the result of the merging of two independent facilities, the former ISG Steel Plant (Indiana Harbor West) and the Ispat-Inland Steel Plant (Indiana Harbor East).

The proposed project would occur on a 0.4-acre parcel on previously disturbed Indiana Harbor East land. The proposed site consists of structural fill placed into Lake Michigan under a series of Army Corps of Engineers fill permits from about 1907 to 1998. Figure 2-2 provides a satellite image of the Indiana Harbor area showing the site boundary and the proposed location of the waste energy recovery facility. Figure 2-3 provides an aerial photograph of the proposed location showing the key existing facilities and proposed new facilities.

Together, the Indiana Harbor West and East sites have five blast furnaces, two sinter plants, a lime plant, three steel shops with six oxygen furnaces and continuous casters, 80- and 84-inch hot-strip mills, two cold-rolling and finishing mills with pickling lines, tandem mills, one aluminizing line, two galvanizing lines, batch and continuous annealing furnaces, and temper mills. Indiana Harbor West and East are capable of producing 10 million tons of steel a year.

Figure 2-1. General location of East Chicago, Indiana.

Indiana Harbor is an integrated mill capable of producing hot-rolled sheet and hot-dipped galvanized sheet metal for use in automotive, appliance, service center, tubular, strip converters, and contractor applications. ArcelorMittal is a major supplier to the North American automotive industry, as well as the broader transportation sector, with customers in the trucking, off-highway, agricultural equipment, and railway industries.

At present, Indiana Harbor uses about 78 percent of its blast furnace gas to preheat the combustion air for the blast furnace and to power boilers; the remaining 22 percent is burned before release to the atmosphere through exhaust stacks, a process called *flaring*. ArcelorMittal's proposed project would convert the waste gas into electricity. The remaining 22 percent (46 billion cubic feet per year) of flared waste gas has an energy content of 4.57 trillion British thermal units per year. The proposed project would use the waste energy to power a new 80-percent efficient boiler to produce 350,000 pounds of steam per hour, and use the additional steam to drive existing turbines to generate electricity. The increase in electricity generation capacity would be about 38 megawatts, which could provide 333,000 megawatt-hours per year. ArcelorMittal would use the electricity for Indiana Harbor operations (ArcelorMittal undated).

The proposed project would include (1) a 17,000-square-foot addition to the existing boilerhouse, (2) 620 feet of new 66-inch pipeline to carry the blast furnace gas from the existing 100-inch diameter blast furnace gas main to the new boiler system, (3) a new feed water system including pumps and deaerator, and (4) a new 290-foot exhaust stack next to the boilerhouse

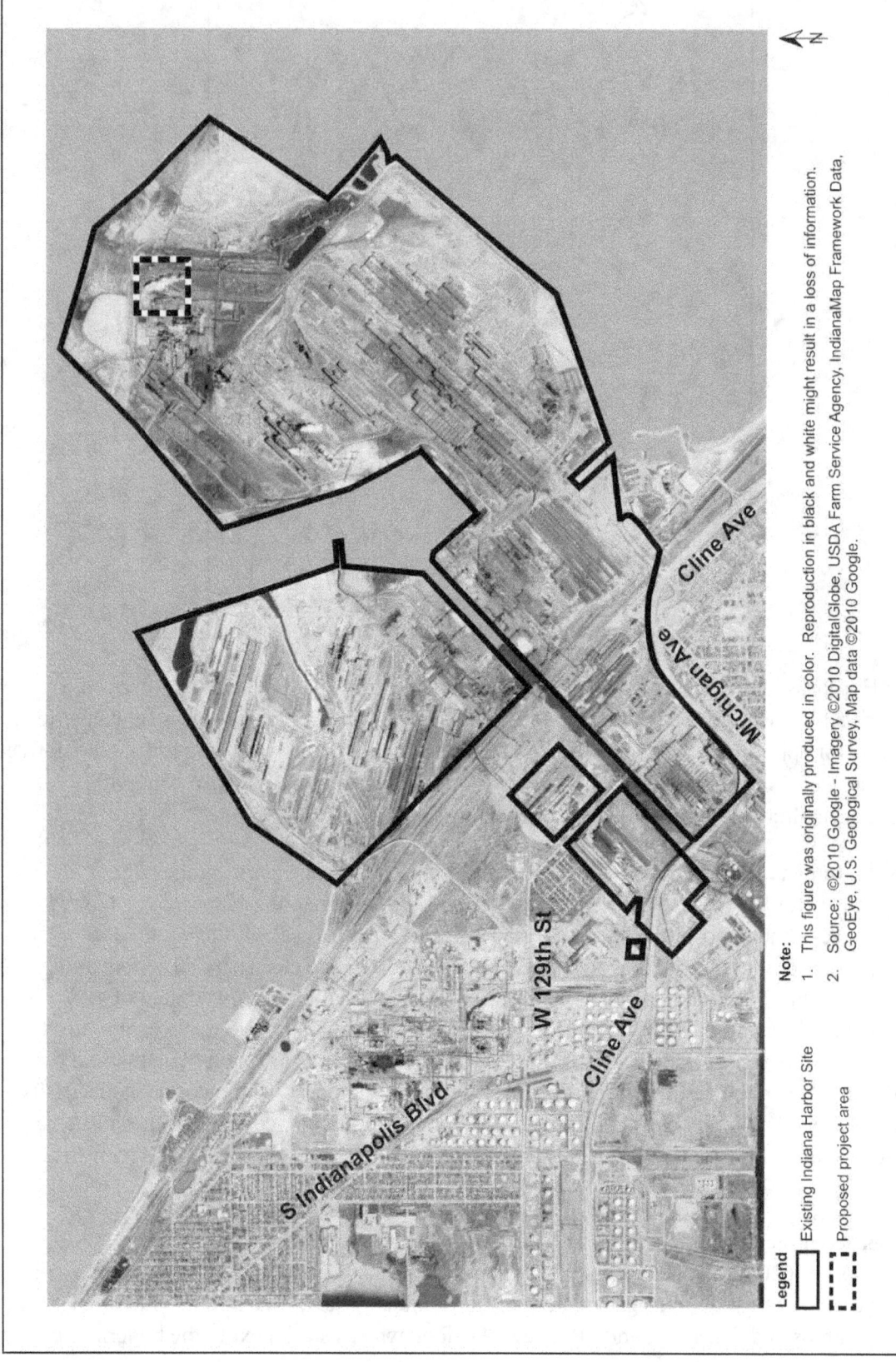

Legend

☐ Existing Indiana Harbor Site

⬚ Proposed project area

Note:
1. This figure was originally produced in color. Reproduction in black and white might result in a loss of information.
2. Source: ©2010 Google - Imagery ©2010 DigitalGlobe, USDA Farm Service Agency, IndianaMap Framework Data, GeoEye, U.S. Geological Survey, Map data ©2010 Google.

Figure 2-2. Satellite view of the Indiana Harbor Steel Mill and vicinity showing the site boundary and location of proposed project.

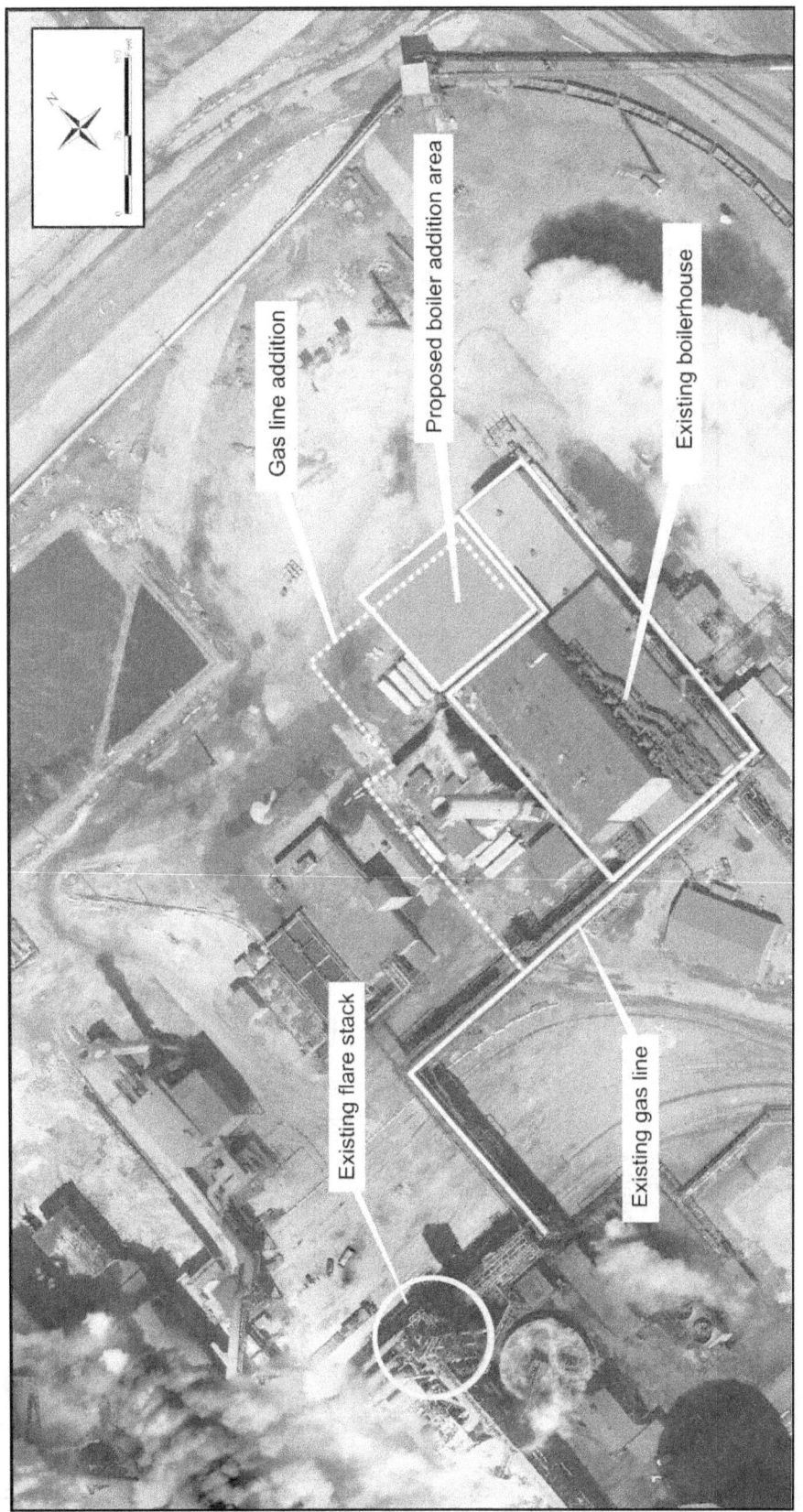

Figure 2-3. Aerial photograph showing existing and proposed facilities.

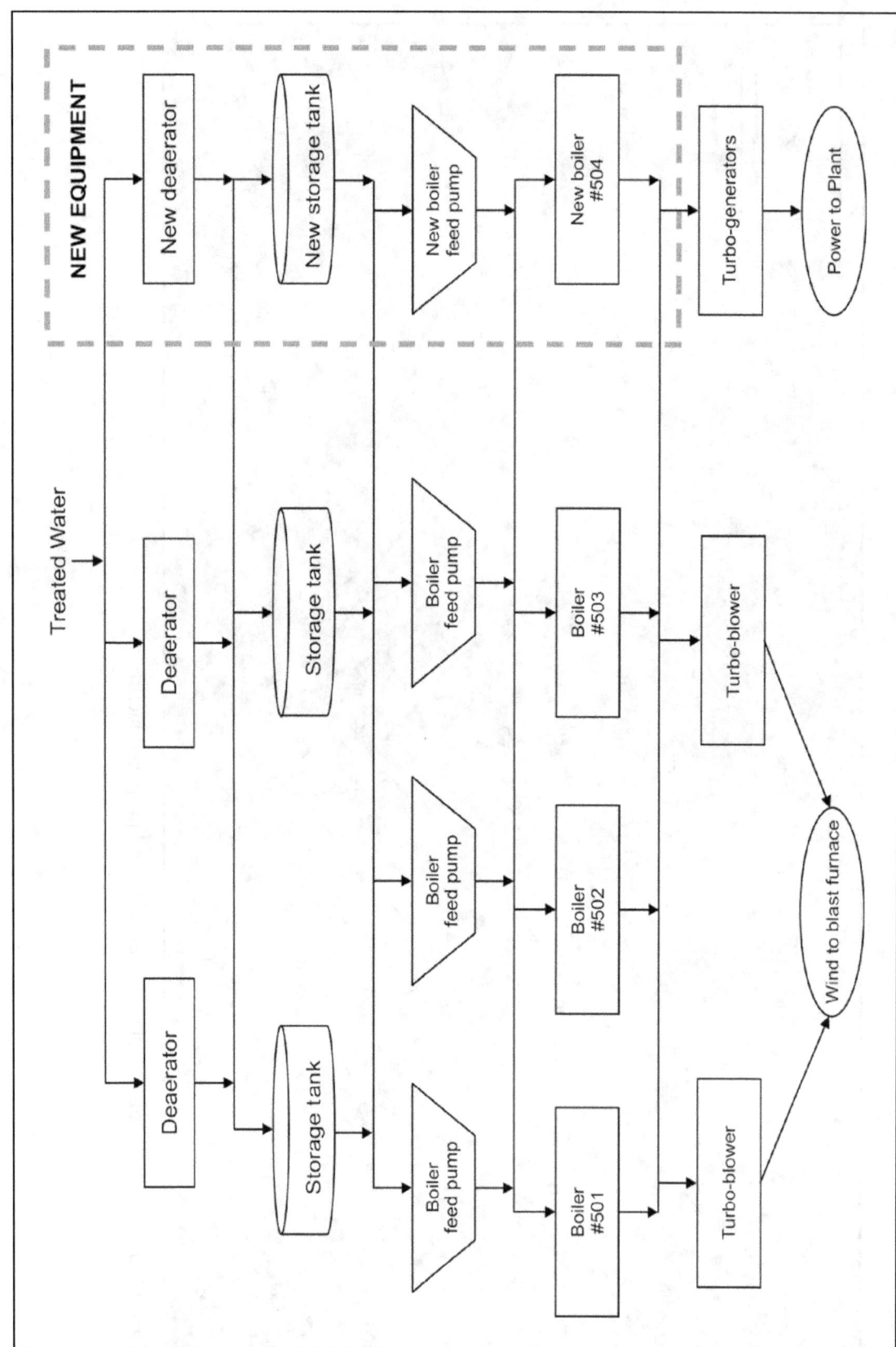

Figure 2-4. Simplified schematic showing existing and proposed facilities.

addition. The project would use the existing site cooling systems and therefore would not require new cooling towers. The proposed project would use the site's existing gas management system to cool and clean the gas for use in the boiler. Figure 2-4 provides a simplified process diagram that shows existing process components and the new elements that would be part of the proposed project.

2.3 No-Action Alternative

Under the No-Action Alternative, DOE would not provide financial assistance for the proposed project. As a result, the project could be delayed as ArcelorMittal sought other funding sources to meet its needs or abandoned if other funding sources could not be obtained. As a result, DOE's ability to achieve its objectives under the Industrial Technologies Program and the Recovery Act would be impaired.

Although this and other selected projects might proceed if DOE decided not to provide financial assistance, the Department assumes for purposes of this environmental analysis that the project would not proceed without its assistance. If ArcelorMittal did proceed without DOE's financial assistance, the potential impacts would be essentially identical to those if the Department provided the funding. To allow a comparison between the potential impacts of a project as implemented and the impacts of not proceeding with a project, DOE assumes that, if it were to decide to withhold assistance from a project, the project would not proceed.

2.4 DOE Alternative Actions

DOE's alternatives to this project consist of the nine technically acceptable applications it received in response to the Funding Opportunity Announcement, *Recovery Act: Deployment of Combined Heat and Power (CHP) Systems, District Energy Systems, Waste Energy Recovery Systems, and Efficient Industrial Equipment* (DE-FOA-0000044). Before selection, DOE made preliminary determinations about the level of review under NEPA based on potentially significant impacts identified during review of the technically acceptable applications. DOE conducted these preliminary reviews pursuant to 10 CFR 1021.216 and a variance to certain requirements in the regulation granted by the Department's General Counsel (74 FR 41963; August 18, 2009). The selection official was provided with these preliminary NEPA determinations and reviews for consideration during the selection process.

Because DOE's Proposed Action is limited to providing financial assistance in cost-sharing arrangements to selected applicants in response to a competitive funding opportunity, DOE's decision is limited to either accepting or rejecting the project as proposed by the proponent, including its proposed technology and selected sites. DOE's consideration of reasonable alternatives is therefore limited to the technically acceptable applications and the No-Action Alternative for each selected project.

3. AFFECTED ENVIRONMENT AND ENVIRONMENTAL CONSEQUENCES

Sections 3.1 to 3.5 detail the affected environment and potential environmental consequences for the proposed project and the No-Action Alternative. The sections discuss air quality, water resources, waste, socioeconomics, and occupational health and safety, respectively. Section 3.6 discusses resource commitments.

3.1 Air Quality

Section 3.1.1 discusses the regional air quality and ArcelorMittal's contributions to the existing baseline conditions. Section 3.1.2 provides a comparison of emissions estimates from current blast furnace operations with those from ArcelorMittal's proposed project.

3.1.1 AFFECTED ENVIRONMENT

The ambient air quality in an area can be characterized in terms of whether it complies with the primary and secondary National Ambient Air Quality Standards. The Clean Air Act (42 U.S.C. 7401 et seq.) requires the U.S. Environmental Protection Agency (EPA) to set national standards for pollutants that are considered harmful to public health and the environment. The EPA established standards for six criteria pollutants: carbon monoxide, lead, nitrogen dioxide, ozone, particulate matter [both with a median aerodynamic diameter of less than or equal to 10 micrometers (PM_{10}) and less than or equal to 2.5 micrometers ($PM_{2.5}$)], and sulfur dioxide. Primary standards define levels of air quality for each of the six criteria pollutants that would provide an adequate margin of safety to protect public health including the health of sensitive populations such as children and the elderly. Secondary standards define levels of air quality that are deemed necessary to protect the public welfare including protection against decreased visibility and damage to animals, crops, vegetation, and buildings. EPA designates regions that do not meet the standards as nonattainment areas. Table 3-1 lists the primary National Ambient Air Quality Standards for each criteria pollutant and the 2008 values for Lake County.

Table 3-1. Primary National Ambient Air Quality Standards and 2008 Lake County air quality.

Pollutant	Averaging period	Primary standard	Lake County 2008
Carbon monoxide	8 hours	9 ppm	3 ppm
	1 hour	35 ppm	7.1 ppm
Lead	Quarterly	1.5 $\mu g/m^3$	0.04 $\mu g/m^3$
Nitrogen dioxide	Annual	0.053 ppm	0.015 ppm
Ozone	8 hours	0.075 ppm	0.068 ppm
PM_{10}	24 hours	150 $\mu g/m^3$	117 $\mu g/m^3$
$PM_{2.5}$	Annual	15.0 $\mu g/m^3$	12.96 $\mu g/m^3$
	24 hour	35 $\mu g/m^3$	32.8 $\mu g/m^3$
Sulfur dioxide	Annual	0.03 ppm	0.015 ppm
	24 hours	0.14 ppm	0.005 ppm

Source: 40 CFR 50.4 through 50.13, EPA 2010.

$\mu g/m^3$ = micrograms per cubic meter; ppm = parts per million.

Figure 3-1 illustrates the general directions and average wind speeds at Chicago's O'Hare International Airport in wind rose format. The prevailing winds are from the southwest. The average regional annual rainfall is about 40 inches a year.

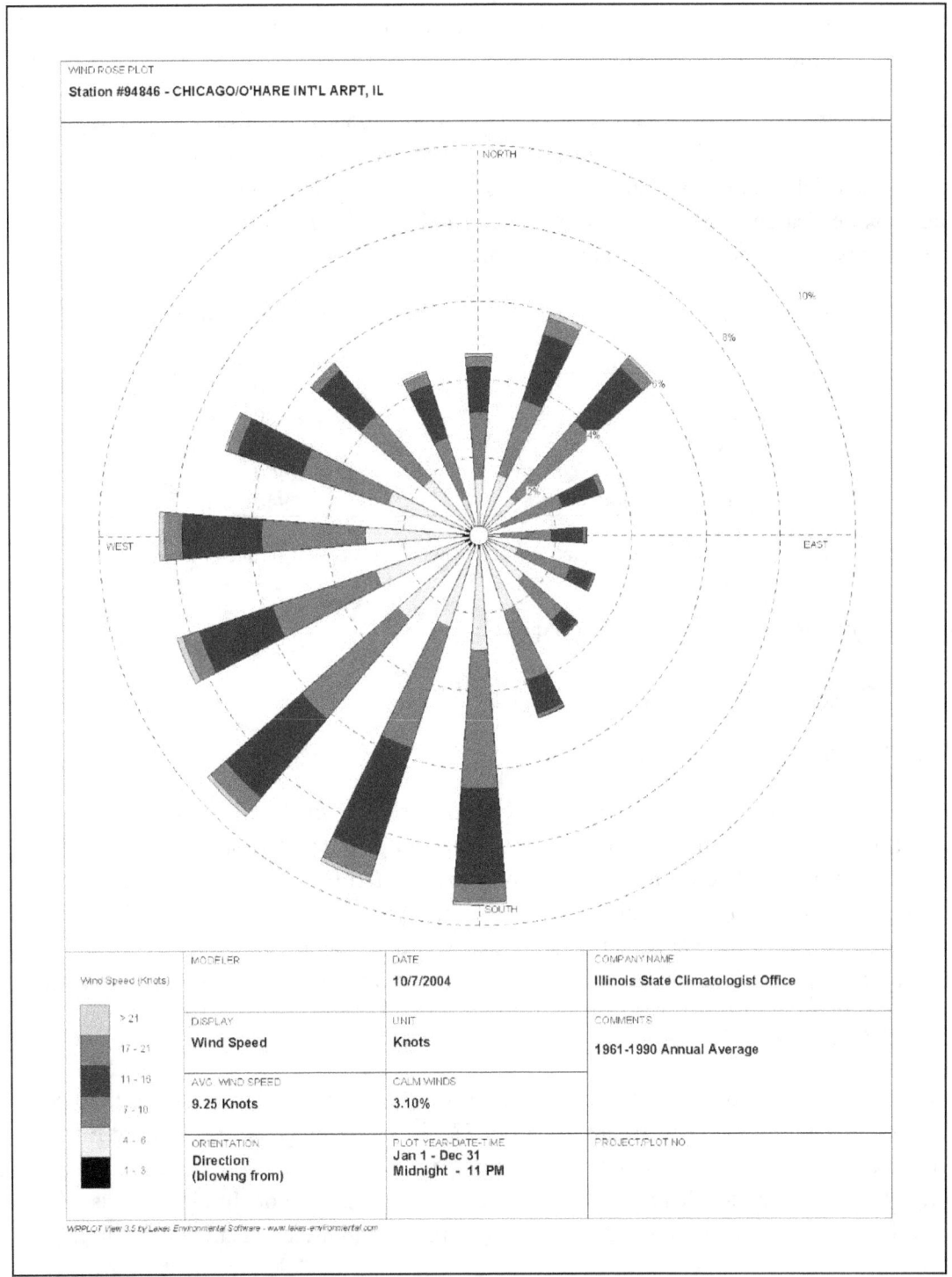

Figure 3-1. O'Hare International Airport wind rose.

The Indiana Harbor Steel Mill is located in Lake County, Indiana, which EPA has designated as in attainment for all criteria pollutants except 8-hour ozone levels (EPA 2010). EPA determined in November 2009 that the Chicago nonattainment area (which includes Lake County) was in attainment of the 1997 $PM_{2.5}$ standard. The Indiana Harbor Steel Mill is designated as a major source for air emissions and has an existing Title V permit under the Clean Air Act. The mill operates below the permitted air emission levels.

The majority of air emissions from current steel mill operations result from the primary end of the integrated iron and steel manufacturing process, which includes blast furnaces, oxygen furnaces, material handling, and process heaters. Table 3-2 summarizes emissions of PM_{10}, nitrogen oxides, carbon monoxide, sulfur dioxide, and volatile organic compounds from combustion based on the current production rate.

Table 3-2. Current Indiana Harbor Steel Mill air emissions (tons per year).

Pollutant	Total emissions
PM_{10}	1,300
Nitrogen oxides	3,600
Carbon monoxide	45,000
Sulfur dioxide	2,400
Volatile organic compounds	940

Source: Seaman 2010b.
PM_{10} = particulate matter with median aerodynamic diameter of 10 micrometers or less.

3.1.2 ENVIRONMENTAL CONSEQUENCES

3.1.2.1 Proposed Project

3.1.2.1.1 *Construction Impacts*

Air emissions from construction activities at the ArcelorMittal steel mill would include combustion emissions from vehicles and heavy-duty equipment and fugitive dust from site preparation activities. These emissions would have short-term adverse impacts that ArcelorMittal could mitigate through best management practices such as soil stabilization and watering of exposed soils. Construction activities would last about 30 months. Fugitive dust emissions would cease on completion of construction, so long-term impacts would be negligible.

3.1.2.1.2 *Operations Impacts*

The proposed project would capture waste blast furnace gas and use it to make steam to generate electricity. At present, ArcelorMittal uses about 78 percent of the gas from the blast furnace to power other mill operations. The remaining 22 percent (46 billion cubic feet per year) is flared before release to the atmosphere. Under the proposed project, ArcelorMittal would use the waste blast furnace gas to create steam to drive existing turbines and thereby generate electricity.

ArcelorMittal is currently finalizing the design of the proposed project, completing operating scenarios, and obtaining estimates of emissions levels for the air permitting process. Based on the currently available information, DOE estimated emissions using emission factors for combustion of blast furnace gas and natural gas, which ArcelorMittal would use to fuel pilot lights for the boiler. Flaring would occur intermittently, typically during start-up of the blast furnace, gas turbine, and boilers; shutdown of the gas turbine; and process transitions. The conversion of waste energy to produce electricity and steam would allow ArcelorMittal to reduce its consumption of electricity from the regional grid, which would result in a reduction in emissions of air pollutants from regional power plants. Table 3-3 lists current emissions estimates for the flare along with emissions estimates for the proposed project.

Table 3-3. Current flare emissions and estimated emissions for the proposed project (tons per year).

Pollutant	Current flare emissions	Proposed project emissions	Change in emissions
PM_{10}	104.1	106.0	1.8
$PM_{2.5}$	104.1	106.0	1.8
Nitrogen oxides	104.1	128.2	24.1
Carbon monoxide	285.4	305.6	20.2
Sulfur dioxide	306.2	306.3	0.1

Source: Seaman 2010b: PM_{10} and $PM_{2.5}$ emissions based on a 1999 stack test; sulfur dioxide emissions based on ArcelorMittal's Title V permit Appendix A; nitrogen oxide emissions based on vendor specification at 3 percent oxygen; carbon monoxide emissions from WebFire database; natural gas combustion emission factors from EPA's *Compilation of Air Pollutant Emission Factors.*

PM_{10} = particulate matter with median aerodynamic diameter of 10 micrometers or less.

$PM_{2.5}$ = particulate matter with median aerodynamic diameter of 2.5 micrometers or less.

The Clean Air Act requires that major air pollution sources undergoing construction or modification comply with all applicable Prevention of Significant Deterioration provisions (40 CFR 52.21) and nonattainment area New Source Review requirements. The Prevention of Significant Deterioration and nonattainment area New Source Review rules require certain analyses before a facility can obtain a permit to begin construction. The Prevention of Significant Deterioration provisions apply to new major sources or major modifications at existing facilities for emission of pollutants in attainment areas for a criteria pollutant. The Prevention of Significant Deterioration regulations require the use of the best available control technology to minimize emissions of pollutants. New Source Review requires companies to obtain permits for new stationary sources of air pollution before beginning construction. New Source Review is also referred to as construction permitting or preconstruction permitting. The proposed project would operate under the incremental provisions of these requirements. ArcelorMittal would comply with applicable emissions limits.

Section 176(c)(1) of the Clean Air Act requires federal agencies to ensure that their actions conform to applicable implementation plans for the achievement and maintenance of the National Ambient Air Quality Standards for criteria pollutants (DOE 2000). To achieve conformity, a federal action must not contribute to new violations of standards for ambient air quality, increase the frequency or severity of existing violations, or delay timely attainment of standards in the area of concern. The EPA general conformity regulations (40 CFR Part 93, Subpart B) contain guidance for determining if a proposed federal action would cause emissions to be above specified levels in nonattainment or maintenance areas.

The plant would operate as an emissions source in accordance with the State of Indiana regulations for individual point source emissions. The Indiana Harbor Steel Mill is located in a nonattainment area for ozone. However, the proposed project would not exceed the threshold emission rate for ozone and would not represent 10 percent or more of the area's emissions inventory for ozone. Therefore, a conformity determination under the Clean Air Act would not be necessary (DOE 2000).

Greenhouse Gas Emissions

The burning of fossil fuels, such as diesel and gasoline, emits carbon dioxide, which is a greenhouse gas. Greenhouse gases can trap heat in the atmosphere and have been associated with global climate change. The Intergovernmental Panel on Climate Change, in *Climate Change 2007: Synthesis Report, Summary for Policy Makers*, stated that warming of the earth's climate system is unequivocal, and that most of the observed increase in globally averaged temperatures since the mid-20th century is very likely due to the observed increase in concentrations of greenhouse gases from human activities (IPCC 2007). Greenhouse gases are well mixed throughout the lower atmosphere, such that any emissions would add to cumulative regional and global concentrations of carbon dioxide.

The project would result in the generation of approximately 330,000 megawatt-hours per year of electric power (enough to serve about 30,000 households) with a net decrease in regional greenhouse gas emissions. Operating the energy-efficient system would result in a decrease in emissions from regional power plants of carbon dioxide emissions. Therefore, DOE expects no cumulative carbon impacts. The conversion of the blast furnace gas to steam to produce electricity would allow ArcelorMittal to reduce its consumption of electricity from regional electric companies, which would result in a reduction in greenhouse gas emissions from regional power plants.

3.1.2.2 No-Action Alternative

Under the No-Action Alternative, DOE would not provide funding to ArcelorMittal for the proposed project, and DOE assumes for analysis in this EA that the project would not proceed without this assistance. ArcelorMittal would continue to purchase most of its electricity from regional utilities and the cogeneration activities at the Indiana Harbor Coke Company. There would be no increase in emissions of pollutants from the ArcelorMittal Steel Mill. There would be no beneficial decrease in regional emissions of pollutants from the use of the energy-efficient system, and the objectives of the Industrial Technologies Program and the Recovery Act would not be advanced.

3.2 Water Resources

Section 3.2.1 discusses current conditions for groundwater, surface water, floodplains, and wetlands. It also discusses ArcelorMittal's use of water and subsequent discharges of wastewater. These discussions form a basis of comparison for the impacts of ArcelorMittal's proposed project in Section 3.2.2.

3.2.1 AFFECTED ENVIRONMENT

3.2.1.1 Surface Water

The Indiana Harbor Steel Mill is located within the Grand Calumet River watershed. The East Branch Grand Calumet River originates in the east end of Gary, Indiana, and flows west through the heavily industrialized cities of Gary and East Chicago. The West Branch originates west of and flows southeast through Hammond, Indiana, to join the East Branch. At this junction, the waters flow north to Lake Michigan through the Indiana Harbor and Ship Canal, which bisects the east and west halves of the steel mill. The majority of the river's flow, about 1 billion gallons per day, drains into Lake Michigan through the Indiana Harbor and Ship Canal. Over 90 percent of the river water is either municipal and industrial effluent or storm water overflow.

The Grand Calumet River and Indiana Harbor and Ship Canal contain 5 to 10 million cubic yards of contaminated sediment from historical sources, many of which no longer exist. Contaminants include toxic compounds (e.g., polychlorinated biphenyls and heavy metals) and conventional pollutants (e.g., phosphorus, nitrogen, iron, magnesium, oil, and grease). Portions of the river, including the Indiana Harbor and Ship Canal, are part of a U.S. Environmental Protection Agency area of concern under the Resource Conservation and Recovery Act (EPA 2009). The Indiana Department of Environmental Management includes most of the river's length as impaired waters under Section 303(d) of the Clean Water Act (33 U.S.C. 1251 et seq.) (IDEM ca. 2008). Chapter 4 discusses the area of concern in relation to the proposed project.

The Indiana Harbor Steel Mill uses water from Lake Michigan, which surrounds the site on three sides, for such purposes as contact and noncontact cooling water, steam production, process gas scrubbing water, and rinse water. Noncontact cooling water does not come into contact with contaminants. The steel mill currently uses about 160 million gallons of water per day from two intakes, one on the north and one on the south of the western portion of the mill. ArcelorMittal treats and discharges about 20 million gallons a day of wastewater, including storm water runoff, and about 100 million gallons per day of noncontact cooling water, to Lake Michigan under a National Pollutant Discharge Elimination System permit. The wastewater from the proposed project would flow to an existing monitored outfall in the northeast corner of the Indiana Harbor and Ship Canal.

3.2.1.2 Groundwater

The regional aquifer is the Calumet Aquifer, which has not been heavily developed because of its proximity to Lake Michigan, an abundant source of surface water. A few domestic and small commercial facilities use the aquifer as a source of water, but ArcelorMittal does not. The City of East Chicago supplies drinking water to the plant.

3.2.1.3 Floodplains and Wetlands

The steel mill is not in a 100-year floodplain, which the Federal Emergency Management Agency designates (HUD 1980). The construction site is part of a parcel of land surrounded on three sides by Lake Michigan. The majority of the steel mill site, including that of the new boiler, consists of manmade fill placed into Lake Michigan from approximately 1907 to 1992. There are no wetlands on the site. Therefore, there would be no impacts to floodplains or wetlands during construction.

3.2.2 ENVIRONMENTAL CONSEQUENCES

3.2.2.1 Proposed Project

3.2.2.1.1 *Construction Impacts*

The two primary water concerns in relation to new construction at the Indiana Harbor Steel Mill would be soil erosion and storm water runoff. The site consists of manmade fill entirely covered by blast furnace slag. All runoff is either directed to onsite swales or collected by the onsite recycling system. ArcelorMittal operates under a National Pollutant Discharge Elimination System storm water discharge permit. Therefore, DOE does not expect significant impacts from soil erosion and storm water runoff.

3.2.2.1.2 *Operations Impacts*

Surface Water

The proposed project would use an estimated 50,000 gallons of water per day from Indiana Harbor Steel Mill's existing intakes in Lake Michigan (Seaman 2010c). ArcelorMittal would treat wastewater from the proposed project in the onsite secondary treatment plant as appropriate. The main source of wastewater would be from using water to clear the boiler of buildup, called *boiler blowdown*, which contains carbonates and scaling materials. ArcelorMittal would treat the blowdown as it does now and combine it with the noncontact cooling water for discharge. ArcelorMittal would continue to pipe sanitary wastewater to the City of East Chicago sanitary treatment system. Wastewater discharges would occur under the existing ArcelorMittal National Pollutant Discharge Elimination System permit. The current permit includes boiler blowdown and would not need modification. Therefore, impacts to surface water quality from normal operations would be unlikely.

Groundwater

The steel mill is not in a 100-year floodplain, as designated by the Federal Emergency Management Agency designates (HUD 1980), and the proposed construction or demolition activities would not occur in a 100-year floodplain. Because the proposed project would be within the existing site boundary, there would be no impacts to existing floodplains. There are no wetlands on the site. Therefore, there would be no impacts to floodplains or wetlands during operations.

Floodplains and Wetlands

The proposed construction or demolition activities would not occur in a 100-year floodplain. Because the proposed project would be within the existing site boundary, there would be no impacts to existing floodplains. There are no wetlands on the site. Therefore, there would be no impacts to floodplains or wetlands during operations.

3.2.2.2 No-Action Alternative

Under the No-Action Alternative, water use and wastewater generation would not increase. DOE does not expect impacts to surface water, groundwater, floodplains, or wetlands.

3.3 Waste

Section 3.3.1 provides the current estimated baseline waste generation for ArcelorMittal's ongoing operations as a basis of comparison for the incremental waste generation from the proposed project in Section 3.3.2.

3.3.1 AFFECTED ENVIRONMENT

ArcelorMittal generates various wastes in the making of steel including wastes from wastewater treatment plants. The treatment plants settle solids from the operations at the mill including the blast furnace, steel shops, hot strip mill, and cold mills. Table 3-4 lists the types and amounts of industrial waste the ArcelorMittal mill currently generates.

Table 3-4. Current Indiana Harbor Steel Mill industrial waste (tons per year).

Type	Amount
Blast furnace and steel shop filter cake	140,000
Water treatment plant sludges	10,000
Mill debris	15,000
Hazardous waste (baghouse dusts)	1,000

Source: Seaman 2010b.

The boilerhouse currently generates miscellaneous municipal wastes (wood, paper, garbage, and absorbents) and a minor amount of hazardous waste from the laboratory at the facility (e.g., caustic and toxic chemicals from water testing) (Seaman 2010d). Boiler wastes consist only of liquid boiler blowdown because the boilers only burn blast furnace gas and natural gas.

The Indiana Harbor Steel Mill operates several aboveground storage tanks. The facility does not use any belowground storage tanks. The mill has a spill prevention and mitigation plan that identifies each tank and describes specific spill control measures. The tanks are distant from the site boundaries (Lake Michigan on three sides), and the mill has a large recycling system to collect oil and water discharges and treat them before discharge through several outfalls permitted under the National Pollutant Discharge Elimination System.

The Indiana Harbor East site is currently complying with a 1993 consent decree that includes requirements for corrective action assessment and cleanup as required. To facilitate this effort, Indiana Harbor East was divided into 14 solid waste management areas. While the proposed project would occur within one of these areas, the proposed site consists of clean structural fill and is not a focus of the ongoing assessment. Section 4.1 provides more information on the consent decree.

3.3.2 ENVIRONMENTAL CONSEQUENCES

3.3.2.1 Proposed Project

3.3.2.1.1 *Construction Impacts*

Construction-related debris would include wood, metal, and concrete. ArcelorMittal would recycle some of this waste and ship the remainder to a permitted commercial landfill in Newton County, Indiana.

3.3.2.1.2 *Operations Impacts*

The characteristics of the waste the proposed project would generate would be similar to current waste streams from the Indiana Harbor Steel Mill. The addition of the proposed boiler and related infrastructure would not significantly increase the amounts of the boilerhouse wastes as described in Section 3.3.1. ArcelorMittal currently disposes of hazardous waste off the site in EPA-permitted facilities and would continue to do so for any new waste streams.

3.3.2.2 No-Action Alternative

Under the No-Action Alternative, waste generation would not increase. Waste levels would remain about the same as those under current operations.

3.4 Socioeconomics

3.4.1 AFFECTED ENVIRONMENT

East Chicago is in Lake County, Indiana. Lake County is part of the Bureau of Census Chicago-Naperville-Joliet, IL-IN-WI Metropolitan Statistical Area. The county's estimated population of 493,800 persons in 2008 reflects a 1.9-percent growth since 2000 (Bureau of the Census 2010). In 2008, the Lake County population was 71.1 percent white, 26.1 percent black, 1.2 percent Asian, and 0.4 percent American Indian or Alaskan Native. About 1.2 percent of the population reported themselves as being of two or more races. Persons of Hispanic or Latino origin made up 14.8 percent of the population (Bureau of the Census 2010).

The county's employment figures reflect the urban nature of the community. The county hosted about 249,000 nonfarming jobs in 2007, of which about 27,000 jobs (11 percent) were in manufacturing (BEA 2010a). In 2000, Lake County residents held about 78 percent of the total jobs (Bureau of the Census 2003). The county's December 2009 labor force had an unemployment rate of 10.3 percent (BLS 2010a).

The 2007 per capita income in Lake County of about $32,000 was 96 percent of the State of Indiana per capita income and about 72 percent of the per capita income in the Chicago-Naperville-Joliet metropolitan statistical area (BEA 2010b). In 2008, about 17 percent of county residents and 13 percent of Indiana residents were living in poverty (Bureau of the Census 2010).

3.4.2 ENVIRONMENTAL CONSEQUENCES

The proposed project would create direct jobs at the ArcelorMittal Indiana Harbor facility during construction and help retain existing jobs during operations. The new construction would create indirect jobs via the multiplier effect, in which the wages workers spend create the need for additional jobs. Additional indirect jobs would include professional, skilled, and unskilled positions; and also would occur among suppliers of goods and services and for the vendors of materials those suppliers would use to fashion goods and services. Earnings by workers in these direct and indirect jobs would generate wages that local, state, and federal governments would tax. In addition, these wages would lead to an increase in banking deposits, which would increase the regional lending base, and to spending on consumable and durable goods and services. The increase in jobs and wages in the community would have a small positive impact.

The current level of employment at the Indiana Harbor Steel Mill, about 4,400 with an additional 1,500 workers on layoff status, is lower than the recent historical job level of 5,400 workers in 2007 (Seaman 2010e). While short-term construction of facilities and the installation of equipment for the proposed project would result in a small increase in jobs, the total workforce in Lake County would remain below previous levels. Therefore, DOE expects that all workers in new positions would be part of the existing labor force in the Chicago-Naperville-Joliet, IL-IN-WI Metropolitan Statistical Area. The additional jobs would be unlikely to cause a noticeable increase in the local population from workers moving into the area. Therefore, impacts to the existing infrastructure, housing, medical care, social services, police and fire protection, schools, or other community services would be unlikely, and DOE does not address these resources further.

3.4.2.1 Proposed Project

3.4.2.1.1 *Construction Impacts*

Preconstruction activities, including design and engineering tasks, procurement of materials, construction of facilities, installation of equipment, and project start-up at Indiana Harbor would take about 30 months (Whalen 2009). Construction would require about 360 directly employed workers. These positions would create about 200 additional indirect jobs. Therefore, the Lake County area would have about 560 new jobs (360 direct and 200 indirect) during construction activities (Seaman 2010f). The 560 jobs would represent about 0.2 percent of the nonfarm employment in Lake County in 2007 (BEA 2010a). The short duration of these positions would result in a smaller indirect effect than that during operations.

ArcelorMittal estimates the cost of preconstruction activities would be $13.1 million, and procurement, construction, and start-up cost would be an additional $50.1 million for a total cost of $63.2 million (ArcelorMittal undated). The estimated total direct earnings would be about $17.2 million. The effect of the total earnings impact by ArcelorMittal would be about $27.4 million in the region. Much of the construction-related spending would directly benefit the suppliers of equipment for the plant and the vendors who would provide materials and services for manufacture of the equipment. The 200 indirect jobs would include employees these companies would retain or hire. Table 3-5 summarizes this information.

Table 3-5. New direct and indirect jobs and earnings effects from construction.

New direct jobs[a]	New indirect jobs[b]	Total new jobs
360	200	560
Earnings effects		
Direct regional infusion $17.2 million	Indirect regional infusion $10.2 million	Total regional infusion $27.4 million

Source: Seaman 2010f.
a. ArcelorMittal jobs.
b. Jobs in the general community.

3.4.2.1.2 *Operations Impacts*

DOE assumed that the proposed project would create no additional new jobs during operations; that is, the Department assumed ArcelorMittal would use existing personnel to operate the proposed waste recovery facility after construction and installation. The savings in electricity costs, however, would help to support the preservation of the nearly 5,900 current workers and help to retain the 26,800 indirect jobs that are dependent on Indiana Harbor expenditures. The direct and indirect jobs would include positions for professional, skilled, and unskilled individuals. The aggregate number of jobs, about 32,600, would have a small positive impact on the labor force by creating job opportunities that could reduce unemployment and increase labor participation. DOE expects that residents of Lake County specifically, and residents of the Chicago-Naperville-Joliet metropolitan area in general, would continue to fill most of the direct and indirect jobs.

The benefits of the proposed project would extend to current Indiana Harbor workers. The anticipated reduction of energy expenses at the facility would improve the company's financial position by reducing per-ton hot metal production costs. This would improve the company's competitiveness and thereby help to preserve about 5,900 skilled jobs in the region's steel industry.

In summary, the operations would create new direct and indirect jobs, aid in the retention of jobs in a critical manufacturing process, and stimulate the economic base of the region. Table 3-6 summarizes this information.

Table 3-6. Retained direct and indirect jobs and earnings effects from operations.

Retained direct jobs[a]	Retained indirect jobs[b]	Total retained jobs
5,900	26,800	32,600
	Earnings effects	
Direct regional infusion	Indirect regional infusion	Total regional infusion
$494 million	$1,400 million	$1,894 million

Source: Seaman 2010f.
a. ArcelorMittal jobs.
b. Jobs in the general region.

3.4.2.2 No-Action Alternative

The No-Action Alternative would result in no short-term jobs during the construction phase of the project and would not improve the potential to retain jobs in the long term. In addition, the objectives of the Industrial Technologies Program and the Recovery Act would not be advanced.

3.5 Occupational Health and Safety

3.5.1 AFFECTED ENVIRONMENT

ArcelorMittal maintains a comprehensive health and safety management program at the Indiana Harbor Steel Mill that would apply to construction and operation of the proposed boiler. Engineering controls are in place to prevent injuries and to control employee exposure to workplace hazards. The company provides comprehensive safety training to new employees and additional periodic training for current workers. ArcelorMittal maintains safety professionals to provide support and direction to Indiana Harbor employees and management.

3.5.2 ENVIRONMENTAL CONSEQUENCES

3.5.2.1 Proposed Project

3.5.2.1.1 *Construction*

The total recordable cases incidence rate in 2008 for nonresidential building construction jobs was 4.3 injuries per 100 full-time employees (BLS 2010b), and the incidence rate for days away from work, days of restricted work activity, or job transfer was 2.2 injuries per 100 full-time employees (BLS 2010c). The estimated construction workforce for this project would be about 361 employees (Section 3.4.2). DOE expects workplace accident rates would be typical of industry averages. Table 3-7 lists estimated numbers of injuries during construction.

Table 3-7. Estimated number of injuries during construction.

Injury category	Estimated annual injuries
On-duty injuries[a]	15.5
Off-duty or restricted-duty injuries[a,b]	7.9

a. Based on 2008 nonresidential building construction industry average of 4.3 on-duty worker injuries per 100 full-time workers.
b. Includes worker injury incidence rate for day away from work and on job transfers; based on 2008 nonresidential building construction industry average of 2.2 off-duty worker injuries per 100 full-time workers.

3.5.1.1.1 *Operations*

The proposed project would be unlikely to result in a deviation from ArcelorMittal's health and safety record. The company maintains and tracks health and safety information on its employees on a regular basis. ArcelorMittal's total Indiana Harbor Occupational Safety and Health

Administration recordable injury rate for 2009 was 4.97 per 200,000 work hours. The current rate for the year to date is up slightly to 5.07 (Seaman 2010g). DOE assumed ArcelorMittal would not hire new employees to operate the proposed boiler; therefore, the proposed project would not contribute to an increase in operational health and safety issues. The Indiana Harbor incident rates are typical at the industry average with variations above and below the industry average.

3.5.1.2 No-Action Alternative

Under the No-Action Alternative, the proposed project would not occur and ArcelorMittal would not hire new employees for construction at the Indiana Harbor Steel Mill. Therefore, there would be no impacts to health and safety.

3.6 Resource Commitments

3.6.1 RELATIONSHIP BETWEEN SHORT-TERM USES OF THE ENVIRONMENT AND THE MAINTENANCE AND ENHANCEMENT OF LONG-TERM PRODUCTIVITY

The construction and operation of a waste energy recovery facility at the Indiana Harbor Steel Mill would result in short-term uses of land. In this context, *short-term use* of resources means the operating life of the mill and *long-term productivity* refers to the period after the mill has ceased operation and undergone decommissioning and demolition. At that time, the land could be occupied and used for other industrial purposes, or it could be reclaimed and revegetated to resemble more natural conditions.

3.6.2 IRREVERSIBLE AND IRRETRIEVABLE COMMITMENTS OF RESOURCES

The use of land as a resource to support the construction and operation of the proposed plant would be irretrievable in the short term. Some unrecyclable construction materials, energy, and the fuel for plant construction and operation would be irreversible and irretrievable commitments of resources. DOE would also have expended funding for the proposed project.

3.6.3 UNAVOIDABLE ADVERSE IMPACTS

The proposed plant would result in the unavoidable small adverse impacts of generating air pollutants and small quantities of waste and wastewater. The small unavoidable impacts would be offset by the positive impact of the conversion of blast furnace waste energy to electricity. This could result in reduced emissions from conventional fossil-fuel generating facilities. There would be short-term increases in noise during the construction period and potential loss of wildlife due to interactions with vehicles or construction equipment.

4. CUMULATIVE IMPACTS

Cumulative impacts result from the incremental effects the proposed project could have in combination with the impacts of past, present, and reasonably foreseeable actions. The proposed project would construct and operate a waste energy recovery facility at the Indiana Harbor Steel Mill, which encompasses about 3,400 acres of land in East Chicago, Indiana. The site has been in use for heavy industry for about 100 years. The East Chicago area has been heavily industrial since the 1890s, with steel mills, refineries, and other heavy industry common to the area. The environmental impacts of past actions have already passed through the environment or are captured as part of the current baseline conditions. The affected environment descriptions, which form the existing baseline conditions for comparison to the incremental impacts of the proposed project, include Indiana Harbor's operational air emissions, water use, and waste generation (Sections 3.1 to 3.3). ArcelorMittal would construct the proposed facility on 0.4 acre of previously disturbed land within the Indiana Harbor Steel Mill site boundary. The proposed site offers sufficient access, onsite roads, and infrastructure to accommodate the new boiler. For most environmental resource areas, there would be no incremental impacts or the impacts would be small, temporary, or both (Section 1.4).

4.1 Present Actions

Indiana Harbor East Consent Decree. In 1990, Inland Steel Company (a predecessor company to ArcelorMittal) was party to a lawsuit filed by EPA under the Resource Conservation and Recovery Act. In 1993, the lawsuit was resolved when Inland Steel Company entered into a consent decree that assessed a fine and required implementation of environmentally beneficial projects at the Indiana Harbor East site. The projects were based on a three-step process for Corrective Action: (1) assessment of the site (including stabilization measures), (2) evaluation of remediation alternatives, and (3) remediation of the site as necessary. The consent decree also required remediation of contaminated sediment for a portion of the Indiana Harbor and Ship Canal (see the section below on the Grand Calumet River Dredging Project). The proposed project in this EA would occur in an area of clean fill and would therefore not affect areas or activities under the consent decree.

Grand Calumet River Area of Concern. The East Branch Grand Calumet River originates in the east end of Gary, Indiana, and flows west through the heavily industrialized cities of Gary and East Chicago, Indiana. The West Branch originates west of and flows southeast through Hammond, where the two branches join and flow north to Lake Michigan. The majority of the river's water, about 1 billion gallons a day, drains into Lake Michigan through the Indiana Harbor and Ship Canal, which bisects the mill site. The area of concern begins 15 miles south of downtown Chicago and includes the East Branch, a small segment of the West Branch, and the Indiana Harbor and Ship Canal. Today, 90 percent of the river's water is from municipal and industrial effluent, cooling and process water, and storm water overflows. Although discharges have been reduced, a number of contaminants continue to impair the area of concern.

The largest impairments come from legacy pollutants in the sediments at the bottom of the Grand Calumet River and Indiana Harbor and Ship Canal. Problems include contamination from polychlorinated biphenyls, polynuclear aromatic hydrocarbons, and heavy metals such as mercury, cadmium, and lead.

The Remediation Action Plan calls for the removal of impairments to beneficial uses of the Grand Calumet River by focusing on aquatic communities, habitats, and sustainable development, which includes restoring aesthetics and recreational use. EPA maintains reports on the status of the remediation efforts as well as efforts to prevent toxic pollution, reduce combined sewer overflows, reduce nonpoint pollution sources, and restore habitat diversity (EPA 2009). See the section below on the Grand Calumet River Dredging Project.

The proposed project would neither contribute to the existing contamination nor impede cleanup activities.

Grand Calumet River Dredging Project. There are corrective actions in the planning and feasibility study stages to dredge the Grand Calumet River to remove contaminants. The current plans call for nearly complete dredging of the canal, and relining the river bottom with gravel, to return the river to a condition which can support benthic (river bottom) aquatic life (EPA 2009). Dredging is scheduled to begin in the fall of 2010. The proposed project would not affect the dredging of the river.

Indiana Harbor Coke Company. Indiana Harbor Coke Company has operated a heat recovery coke production plant since 1998 on the Indiana Harbor Steel Mill site. The plant produces 1.3 million tons of coke from 268 ovens. The coke company uses a conveyor to send the coke to ArcelorMittal's blast furnace. Waste heat from the coking process goes to Primary Energy's cogeneration plant, which converts it to process steam and electricity for use at the mill (SunCoke 2006). The coke plant uses 17,000 gallons of water per day, but 3,000 gallons evaporate into the air and 14,000 gallons are for cooling, so there are no net wastewater discharges. The coke plant operations include the ovens, four pusher-charger machines, four hot cars that carry the coal to and from the ovens, two conventional wet quench stations that cool the coal, coal silos, computer-controlled coke wharves, and control rooms. DOE does not expect that the proposed construction and operation of a combined-cycle power generation plant on the ArcelorMittal site would reduce or alter the availability of water withdrawals from Lake Michigan. The Indiana Harbor Coke Company currently uses less than 0.01 percent of ArcelorMittal use on a daily basis, and the proposed project would not affect this amount. The incremental increases in criteria air pollutants also would have a negligible effect on the regional air quality.

4.2 Reasonably Foreseeable Actions

Whiting Refinery Modernization Project. The British Petroleum Whiting Refinery Modernization Project in Whiting, Indiana, includes the construction of a new coker, crude distillation unit, gas-oil hydrotreater, and sulfur recovery facilities. When complete in 2011 or 2012, the project will increase the refinery's gasoline production by 1.7 million gallons a day. The refinery is about 5 miles west of ArcelorMittal's proposed project site. The modernization includes a number of environmental improvements such as modernized water treatment facilities. The refinery will operate within more stringent discharge limits for ammonia and suspended solids than the refinery's current water discharge permit allows (BP 2008). There could be very small incremental increases in water use and criteria air pollutants from the refinery, but these would have negligible effects in combination with ArcelorMittal's proposed project.

Cumulative impact considerations, as described above, would result in very small incremental contributions from the proposed operations at Indiana Harbor as described in Chapter 3 and summarized in Chapter 5.

5. CONCLUSIONS

ArcelorMittal proposes to construct and operate a waste energy recovery facility on the site of its Indiana Harbor Steel Mill in East Chicago, Indiana. The company would construct the facility on 0.4 acre of previously disturbed land on the 3,400-acre steel mill site.

In this EA, DOE considered:

1. The Proposed Action of providing a Recovery Act financial assistance grant in a cost-sharing arrangement with ArcelorMittal,

2. ArcelorMittal's proposed project to capture blast furnace flare gas and process the waste energy into electricity, and

3. The No-Action Alternative.

The analyses for this EA considered all the environmental resource areas DOE typically includes in NEPA documents. Nine of the 14 environmental resource areas were not carried forward for more detailed analyses because DOE determined there would be no impacts or the potential impacts would be small or temporary in nature, or both. Consequently, DOE focused its detailed analyses on those resource areas that would require new or amended permits, have the potential for significant impacts or controversy, or would typically interest the public, such as socioeconomics and occupational health and safety. These resource areas included:

- Air quality,
- Water resources,
- Waste,
- Socioeconomics, and
- Occupational health and safety.

In addition, DOE consulted with the Indiana Division of Historic Preservation and Archaeology as required by Section 106 of the National Historic Preservation Act. The Department determined there would be no historic properties affected, and the Indiana Deputy State Historic Preservation Officer concurred with DOE's determination (See Appendix B).

DOE also reviewed the list of federally threatened and endangered species and their habitat requirements in Lake County, Indiana. The Department determined there would be no effect on threatened or endangered species. DOE received telephone concurrence from the Midwest Region FWS office (Craig 2010) about the species list and concurrence with DOE's determination of no effect.

The proposed project would potentially have beneficial impacts that resulted from recovering waste energy and converting it into electricity for use at the steel mill. This would allow ArcelorMittal to purchase less electricity from regional power plants and potentially reduce pollutant emissions from conventional generating sources that use fossil fuels.

Air emissions during construction for the proposed project at the Indiana Harbor Steel Mill would include combustion emissions from vehicles and heavy-duty equipment and fugitive dust from site preparation activities. These emissions would have short-term adverse impacts that ArcelorMittal could mitigate through best management practices such as soil stabilization and watering of exposed soils. Fugitive dust emissions would cease on completion of construction, so long-term impacts would be negligible.

Air emissions from the proposed project operations would remain about the same as current emissions, with the exception of minimal increases in nitrogen oxides and carbon monoxide. The proposed project would generate about 330,000 megawatt-hours per year of electricity (enough to serve about 30,000 households), with a slight increase of greenhouse gas emissions on the site.

The Indiana Harbor Steel Mill is located within the Grand Calumet River watershed. Portions of the river, including the Indiana Harbor and Ship Canal that bisects the steel mill, are part of a U.S. Environmental Protection Agency area of concern under the Resource Conservation and Recovery Act. Chapter 4 discusses the area of concern as part of the cumulative impact analysis.

The proposed project would use water from Indiana Harbor Steel Mill's existing intakes in Lake Michigan. ArcelorMittal would treat wastewater in the existing onsite secondary treatment plant as appropriate. The main source of wastewater would be from boiler blowdown, which contains carbonates and scaling materials. The proposed project would have a small impact on the quantity of wastewater the steel mill discharges into the Grand Calumet River, and there would be no change in the quality of that wastewater. The current ArcelorMittal National Pollutant Discharge Elimination System permit would not require modification.

ArcelorMittal would not use groundwater for operations and there would be no underground storage tanks for the proposed project. Therefore, impacts to groundwater availability and quality would be unlikely from normal operations. ArcelorMittal would prevent or mitigate potential impacts from accidental spills of contaminants by following a spill prevention and mitigation plan.

None of the proposed construction activities would occur in a 100-year floodplain, and there are no wetlands on the site. DOE anticipates no impacts to floodplains and wetlands.

Construction for the proposed project would generate construction-related debris such as wood, metal, and concrete. ArcelorMittal would recycle some of this waste and ship the remainder to a permitted commercial landfill in Newton County, Indiana. During normal operations, ArcelorMittal would generate miscellaneous municipal wastes (for example, wood, paper, garbage, and absorbents) and a minor amount of hazardous waste (caustic and toxic chemicals from water testing) from the laboratory at the facility that would not affect regional landfills or treatment plants.

The proposed project would have the beneficial impact of creating new direct and indirect jobs during construction, aiding in the retention of jobs in a critical manufacturing process, and stimulating the economic base of the community. DOE expects that members of the community's existing labor force would fill the new jobs, so there would be no adverse impacts to the existing infrastructure or social services.

ArcelorMittal maintains a comprehensive health and management system at the Indiana Harbor Steel Mill. DOE expects (1) that the workplace accident rates during the construction period would be typical of industry averages and (2) that the operations workforce would have accident rates similar to ArcelorMittal's historical health and safety record. ArcelorMittal's total recordable injury rate at Indiana Harbor has consistently been near the industry average with slight variations above and below that average.

Cumulative impact considerations included remediation activities at Indiana Harbor and for the Grand Calumet River and the Indiana Harbor and Ship Canal; operations of the Indiana Harbor Coke Company; and the modernization of the British Petroleum Whiting Refinery. DOE determined there would be no or minimal incremental cumulative impacts to the environment or human health and safety from the proposed project in combination with these other projects.

In terms of the No-Action Alternative, DOE assumed ArcelorMittal would not proceed with the project without DOE assistance. Therefore, there would be no impacts to any resource category. However, the above-described potential for positive impacts to air quality and socioeconomics would also not occur. In addition, DOE's ability to achieve its objectives under the Industrial Technologies Program and the Recovery Act would be impaired.

6. REFERENCES

ArcelorMittal USA, undated, *Project Summary/Abstract*, East Chicago, Indiana.

BEA (Bureau of Economic Analysis), 2010a, "Table CA25N-Total full-time and part-time employment by NAICS industry, Lake County, Indiana, 2007," U.S. Department of Commerce, Washington, D.C., accessed March 2, 2010. http://www.bea.gov/regional/reis/

BEA (Bureau of Economic Analysis), 2010b, "Table CA1-3 Per Capita Personal Income, Indiana, 2007," U.S. Department of Commerce, Washington, D.C., accessed March 2, 2010. http://www.bea.gov/regional/reis/

BLS (Bureau of Labor Statistics), 2010a, "Local Area Unemployment Statistics, Lake County, Indiana, 2009" U.S. Department of Labor, Washington, D.C., accessed April 28, 2010. http://data.bls.gov/cgi-bin/dsrv

BLS (Bureau of Labor Statistics), 2010b, "Occupational Injuries and Illnesses, Industry Data, Nonresidential building construction, total recordable cases, 2008" U.S. Department of Labor, Washington, D.C., accessed April 27, 2010. http://data.bls.gov/cgi-bin/dsrv

BLS (Bureau of Labor Statistics), 2010c, "Occupational Injuries and Illnesses, Industry Data, Nonresidential building construction, Cases involving days away from work, job restriction, or transfer, 2008" U.S. Department of Labor, Washington, D.C., accessed April 27, 2010. http://data.bls.gov/cgi-bin/dsrv

BP (BP America), 2008, "Whiting Refinery Modernization Project Moving into High Gear," July 29, accessed May 25, 2010. http://www.bp.com/genericarticle.do?categoryId=2012968&contentId=7046513

Bureau of Census, 2003, "Residence County to Workplace County Flows for Indiana, Sorted by Workplace State and County," U.S. Department of Commerce, Washington, D.C., March 6, accessed April 26, 2010. http://www.census.gov/population/www/cen2000/commuting/index.html.

Bureau of Census, 2010, "State and County QuickFacts, Indiana and Lake County, Indiana," U.S. Department of Commerce, Washington, D.C., February 23, accessed February 24, 2010. http://quickfacts.census.gov/qfd/states/18/18089.html

Craig, B., 2010, "Threatened and Endangered Species at the ArcelorMittal Indiana Harbor Steel Mill, East Chicago, Lake County, Indiana," note to file, Dade Moeller & Associates, Richland, Washington, May 19.

DOE (U.S. Department of Energy), 2000, *Clean Air Act General Conformity Requirements and the National Environmental Policy Act Process*, Office of Environment, Safety and Health, Washington, D.C., April.

EPA (U.S. Environmental Protection Agency), 2009, "Grand Calumet River Area of Concern," Washington, D.C., August 31, accessed April 26, 2010. http://www.epa.gov/glnpo/aoc/grandcal.htm

EPA (U.S. Environmental Protection Agency), 2010, "County Air Quality Report -- Criteria Air Pollutants, Geographic Area: Lake Co, IN, Year: 2008," Washington, D.C., accessed May 25, 2010. http://www.epa.gov

FWS (U.S. Fish and Wildlife Service), 2010, *County Distribution of Indiana's Federally Threatened, Endangered, Proposed and Candidate Species*, Indiana Field Office, Columbus, Indiana, November.

HUD (U.S. Department of Housing and Urban Development), 1980, *Firm, Flood Insurance Rate Map, City of East Chicago, Indiana, Lake County, Community-Panel Numbers 180130 0001·0006, Federal Insurance Administration*, Washington, D.C., June 4, accessed March 9, 2010. http://msc.fema.gov

IDEM (Indiana Department of Environmental Management), ca. 2008, "2008 303(d) List of Impaired Waters," Indianapolis, Indiana, accessed May 17, 2010. http://www.in.gov/idem/4680.htm

IPCC (Intergovernmental Panel on Climate Change), 2007, *Climate Change 2007: Synthesis Report, Summary for Policy Makers*, Geneva, Switzerland.

Seaman, J. T., 2010a, "Re: FW:," e-mail to B. Craig (Dade Moeller & Associates), ArcelorMittal USA, East Chicago, Indiana, April 16.

Seaman, J. T., 2010b, "Fw:," e-mail to B. Craig (Dade Moeller & Associates), ArcelorMittal USA, East Chicago, Indiana, April 7.

Seaman, J. T., 2010c, "Fw: Follow-up of Draft EA and Draft Ad," e-mail to B. Craig (Dade Moeller & Associates), ArcelorMittal USA, East Chicago, Indiana, May 28.

Seaman, J. T., 2010d, "FW: Quick Question," e-mail to B. Craig (Dade Moeller & Associates), ArcelorMittal USA, East Chicago, Indiana, April 26.

Seaman, J. T., 2010e, "FW: 504 Boiler - DOE funded project," e-mail to B. Craig (Dade Moeller & Associates), ArcelorMittal USA, East Chicago, Indiana, April 19.

Seaman, J. T., 2010f, "Re: ArcelorMittal EA," e-mail to B. Craig (Dade Moeller & Associates), ArcelorMittal USA, East Chicago, Indiana, March 8.

Seaman, J. T., 2010g, "FW: 504 Boiler - DOE funded project - Safety Questions," e-mail to B. Craig (Dade Moeller & Associates), ArcelorMittal USA, East Chicago, Indiana, April 19.

SunCoke Energy, 2006, "About SunCoke Energy," accessed May 25, 2010. http://www.suncoke.com/existingprojects.html

Whalen, M. D., 2009, "U.S. Department of Energy Environmental Questionnaire," ArcelorMittal USA, East Chicago, Indiana, July 10.

APPENDIX A
DISTRIBUTION LIST

Mr. Brad Baughn
Business in Legislative Liaison
100 North Senate Avenue, Room 13.0
Indianapolis, Indiana 46204

The Honorable Mitchell E. Daniels, Jr.
Governor of Indiana
Office of the Governor
Indianapolis, Indiana 460204-2797

Commissioner Thomas W. Easterly
Indiana Government Center North
100 North Senate Avenue
Indianapolis, Indiana 46204

Mr. James Glass
Indiana Division of Historic Preservation and Archeology
402 West Washington Street
Indianapolis, Indiana 46204

Mr. Kevin Haggerty
U.S. Department of Energy
Freedom of Information Act Reading Room
1000 Independence Avenue, SW, 1-G-033
Washington, D.C. 20585

The Honorable Earl Harris
Representative, Indiana House of Representatives
200 West Washington Street
Indianapolis, Indiana 46204-2786

Indiana Harbor Coke Company
3210 Watling Street
East Chicago, Indiana 46312

The Honorable George Pabey
Mayor of East Chicago
4527 South Indianapolis Boulevard
East Chicago, Indiana 46312-3226

Mr. David Perry
NEPA Coordinator
Indiana Department of Environmental Management
100 North Senate Avenue
Indianapolis, Indiana 46204

Mr. David Pippen, Indiana Commissioner
Policy Director for Environment & Natural Resources
Office of the Governor
Indiana State House, Room 206
Indianapolis, Indiana 46204

Mr. Scott Pruitt
U.S. Fish and Wildlife Service
620 South Walker Street
Bloomington, Indiana 47403-2121

The Honorable Lonnie Randolph
Senator, Indiana State Senate
200 West Washington Street
Indianapolis, Indiana 46204-2785

Mr. John T. Seaman
Project Manager
ArcelorMittal USA
3210 Watling Street
M.C. 8-136
East Chicago, Indiana 46312

Mr. Kenneth Westlake
Supervisor, NEPA Implementation
Office of Enforcement and Compliance Assurance
U.S. Environmental Protection Agency, Region 5
77 West Jackson Boulevard, Mail Code E-19J
Chicago, Illinois 60604-3590

Ms. Jo Ann Yuill
U.S. Department of Energy
National Environmental Technology Laboratory Reading Room
P.O. Box 10940
Pittsburgh, Pennsylvania 15236

APPENDIX B
CONSULTATIONS

This appendix contains a copy of the consultation letter from DOE to the Indiana Division of Historic Preservation and Archaeology and a copy of the Division's response.

 **NATIONAL ENERGY TECHNOLOGY LABORATORY**
Albany, OR · Morgantown, WV · Pittsburgh, PA

 **U.S. DEPARTMENT OF ENERGY**

March 17, 2010

Mr. James Glass
Director
Division of Historic Preservation & Archaeology
200 Washington Street
Indianapolis, Indiana 46204

Dear Mr. Glass:

The U.S. Department of Energy (DOE or the Department) is proposing to provide a financial grant to ArcelorMittal USA, Inc., as part of the Industrial Technologies Program funded through the *American Recovery and Reinvestment Act of 2009* (Recovery Act). If funded, ArcelorMittal would construct and operate a waste recovery boiler that would capture the gas flare from the blast furnace at ArcelorMittal's Indian Harbor Steel Mill to generate steam (the proposed undertaking). The steam would be used to generate electricity. The new power generating plant would be collocated at ArcelorMittal's Indian Harbor site and would involve approximately 0.4 of an acre on lands previously disturbed and currently graveled. The existing 3,398 acre Indian Harbor Steel Mill site is located at 3210 Watling Street, East Chicago, Lake County, Indiana.

The attachment provides a summary of information that is typically required for Section 106 reviews under the *National Historic Preservation Act*. The attached Figures 1 through 3 provide supporting maps and a photograph.

Based on internal scoping, DOE has identified the following properties that are listed in the *National Register of Historic Places* within East Chicago, Lake County, Indiana.

Name	Address	Reference No.	City	County
Indian Harbor Public Library	3005 Grand Avenue	05001014	East Chicago	Lake
Marktown Historic District	Bounded by Riley, Dickey, and 129th Streets	75000025	East Chicago	Lake

Reference numbers are from the National Register database at http://www.nps.gov/nr/research/index.htm.

Given the geographic location of the proposed project in relation to known historic properties and that the area of direct potential effects would be limited to a 0.4-acre parcel of previously disturbed land within ArcelorMittal's Indian Harbor Steel Mill site boundary; no direct impacts to historic properties are anticipated. Concerning indirect impacts, potential construction noise would be temporary, and additional noise from operations would not increase plant ambient noise beyond existing levels. From a visual resources standpoint, views from within the site, or from outside the site boundary, would not result in major changes to the existing visual characteristics of the site.

Based on DOE's analysis as documented in this letter and its attachments, DOE has determined that no historic properties will be affected by this proposed project. In compliance with 36 CFR Part 800.4(d)

3610 Collins Ferry Road, P.O. Box 880, Morgantown, WV 26507

(1), the Department asks the Division of Historic Preservation & Archaeology for its concurrence of this finding.

DOE's National Energy Technology Laboratory is preparing a draft environmental assessment (EA) for this project. DOE will include correspondence with your office in an appendix to the EA. DOE will send you a copy of the draft EA and respond to any specific comments you may have. At this time, we anticipate implementing a 15-day public comment period for this proposed project.

Please forward the results of your review and any requests for additional information to Mark Lusk of the Department's National Energy Technology Laboratory using the contact information provided in the attached form. Since this is a Recovery Act project, we would appreciate a quick response to our request for consultation. If you have any questions or require clarification, please contact me at (304) 285-4145 or at mark.lusk@netl.doe.gov. Thank you in advance for your consideration.

Sincerely,

Mark W Lusk

Mark Lusk
Document Manager

Attachments
Figures 1 to 3

ATTACHMENT

**U.S. Department of Energy Proposed Funding to ArcelorMittal USA, Inc.
For a Blast Furnace Gas Flare Capture Project at ArcelorMittal's Indian Harbor Works,
East Chicago, Indiana**

1. Responsible Federal Agency and Contact Information:

   U.S. Department of Energy
   Mr. Mark W. Lusk
   Document Manger
   3610 Collins Ferry Road, P.O., Box 880 MS B07
   Morgantown, WV 26507-0880
   Phone 304-285-4145; e-mail mark.lusk@netl.doe.gov

2. Description of the Undertaking:

ArcelorMittal's proposed project would install and operate a waste recovery boiler that would capture and utilize 46 billion cubic feet of blast furnace gas per year to generate electricity. This gas is currently wasted when flared into the atmosphere, . The boiler would be collocated at ArcelorMittal's Indian Harbor Steel Mill on Lake Michigan in East Chicago, Lake County, Indiana. The site address is 3210 Watling Street, East Chicago, Indiana. Figure 1 provides a street map of the area.

The Indian Harbor site has been used for heavy industry for over a hundred years. The Indian Harbor facility comprises 3,398 acres; the proposed project would expand the footprint of the No. 5 boiler house by 0.4 of an acre on previously disturbed, graveled land. Figure 2 provides a satellite image of the entire site with the approximate location of the construction area noted.

ArcelorMittal's proposed project would convert waste blast furnace gas, a byproduct of the iron- and steel-making process that is currently flared into the atmosphere, into electricity. Presently, approximately 78 percent of the blast furnace gas that is generated is used by the mill. The remaining 22 percent (46 billion cubic feet per year) is wasted. The wasted gas has an energy content of 4.57 trillion Btu per year. The proposed project would fire the waste gas through a new 80-percent efficient boiler to produce 350,000 pounds of steam per hour. The net increase in self-generation would be 38 megawatts of electricity, or 333,000 megawatt-hours per year. The electricity would be used on the site. Figure 3 shows an aerial photograph of the existing facility and the footprint of the expanded boiler house.

3. Area of Potential Effects (APE):

   The APE is the 0.4 acre of previously disturbed land that would be used to expand the existing No. 5 boiler house as shown on Figure 3.

4. U.S. Geological Survey Quad, Aerial Photos, Plat:

   With regard to the APE, see Figures 2 to 3. Additionally, the APE and the Indian Harbor site can be found on the USGS Whiting Quadrangle (7-1/2 minute), at 41° 40" north latitude, 87° 27" west longitude.

5.   Construction Dates and Known Historical Significance:

The proposed site and APE are on previously disturbed land, currently vacant of any buildings or support structures. Overall, the site of the Indian Harbor Steel Mill has been in continuous use as a heavy-industry site for well over 100 years. Although there are buildings and structures that may exceed 50 years in age, none are known to have any historical significance; all have served steel or iron production for many years.

6.   Condition of Vacant Land.

The proposed construction site, which is identified as the APE, is previously disturbed land, currently graveled. Refer to Figures 2 and 3.

7.   Other Information.

DOE is preparing an environmental assessment (EA) that will be issued as a draft in the next few months. The availability of the Draft EA will be announced in the local newspaper of record and a copy placed in the local library. DOE will solicit and accept comments by mail, facsimile, or e-mail during the public comment period which will be announced in the EA availability notice.

At this time DOE has no plans to formally consult with any other federal or state agency or American Indian tribe. However, DOE is developing a distribution list for the EA. The distribution list will include appropriate local, state, and other federal agencies, members of the public that have expressed an interest in the project, and any interested environmental or historic preservation groups.

Figure 1. General street map showing the location of ArcelorMittal's Indian Harbor Steel Mill.

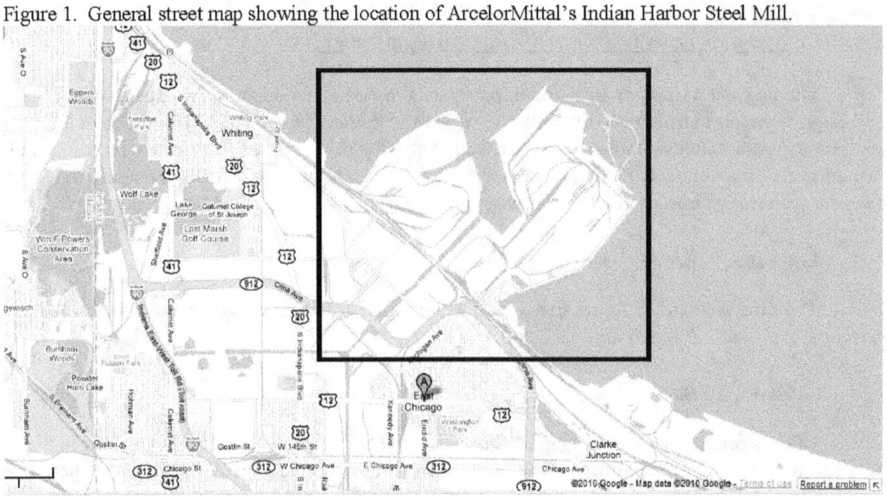

Figure 2. Indian Harbor site map showing general location of the proposed undertaking (thick black box).

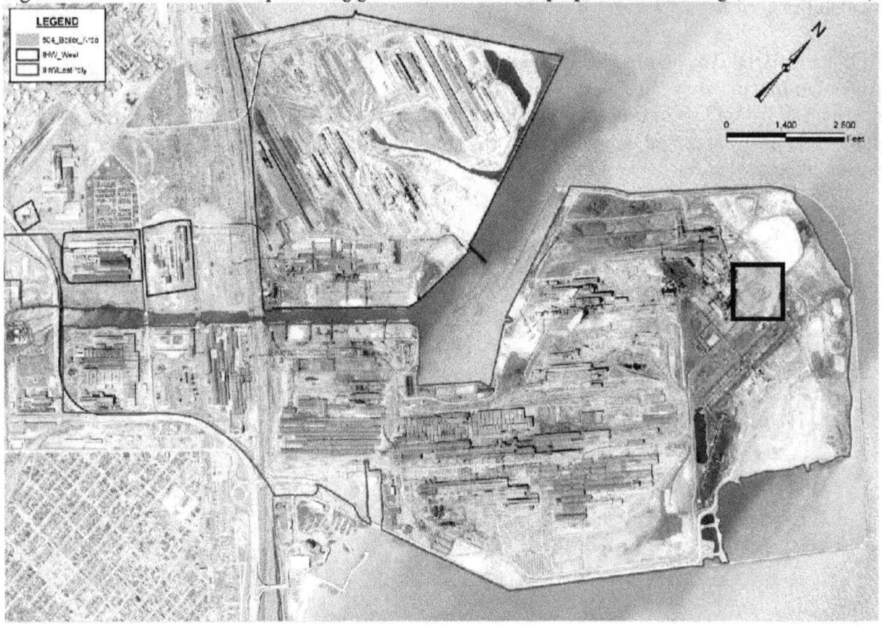

Figure 3. Aerial view of existing facility showing proposed project details.

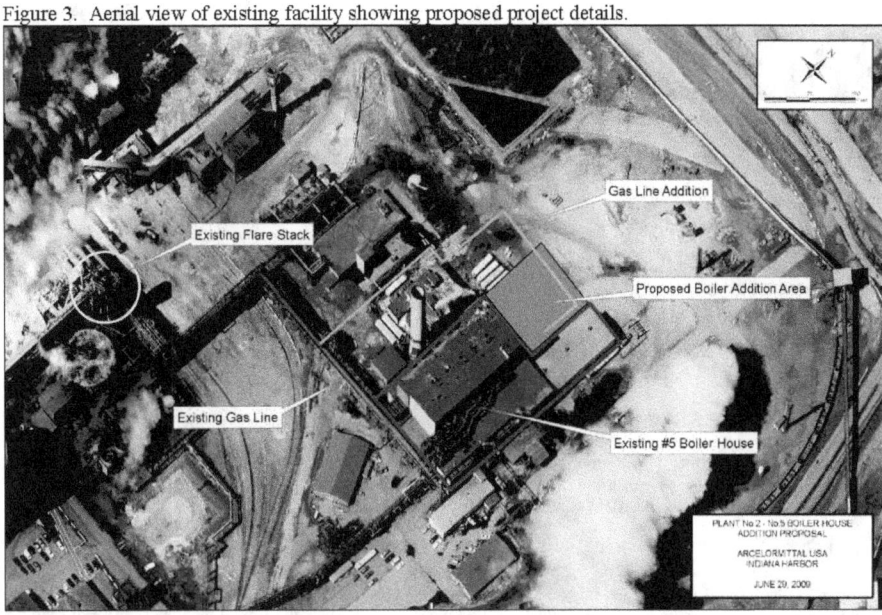

Mitchell E. Daniels, Jr., Governor
Robert E. Carter, Jr., Director

DNR Indiana Department of Natural Resources

Division of Historic Preservation & Archaeology•402 W. Washington Street, W274 · Indianapolis, IN 46204-2739
Phone 317-232-1646•Fax 317-232-0693 · dhpa@dnr.IN.gov

April 19, 2010

Mark Lusk
Document Manager
U.S. Department of Energy
P.O. Box 880 MS B07
Morgantown, WV 26507-0880

Federal Agency: U.S. Department of Energy

Re: Project information and notification of the U.S. Department of Energy's finding of "no historic properties affected" regarding installation of a waste recovery boiler at ArcelorMittal's Indian Harbor Steel Mill located at 3210 Watling Street (DHPA #9338)

Dear Mr. Lusk:

Pursuant to Section 106 of the National Historic Preservation Act (16 U.S.C. § 470f) and 36 C.F.R. Part 800, the staff of the Indiana State Historic Preservation Officer ("Indiana SHPO") has conducted an analysis of the materials dated March 17, 2010 and received on March 23, 2010, for the above indicated project in East Chicago, Lake County, Indiana.

We concur with the U.S. Department of Energy's March 17, 2010 finding that there are no historic buildings, structures, districts, objects, or archaeological resources within the area of potential effects that will be affected by the above indicated project.

This identification is subject to the following condition:

- The project activities remain within areas disturbed by previous construction.

If any archaeological artifacts or human remains are uncovered during construction, demolition, or earthmoving activities, state law (Indiana Code 14-21-1-27 and 29) requires that the discovery must be reported to the Department of Natural Resources within two (2) business days. In that event, please call (317) 232-1646. Be advised that adherence to Indiana Code 14-21-1-27 and 29 does not obviate the need to adhere to applicable federal statutes and regulations.

If you have questions about archaeological issues please contact Amy Johnson at (317) 232-6982 or ajohnson@dnr.IN.gov. If you have questions about buildings or structures please contact Ashley Thomas at (317) 234-7034 or asthomas@dnr.IN.gov.

Very truly yours,

James A. Glass, Ph.D.
Deputy State Historic Preservation Officer

JAG:ADT:ALJ:aj

An Equal Opportunity Employer
Printed on Recycled Paper

www.ingramcontent.com/pod-product-compliance
Lightning Source LLC
Chambersburg PA
CBHW081228170526
45165CB00009B/2994